FINDING
BALANCE
POETRY

PALMETTO
PUBLISHING
Charleston, SC
www.PalmettoPublishing.com

Copyright © 2024 by Miss Q

All rights reserved

No portion of this book may be reproduced, stored in a retrieval system, or transmitted in any form by any means–electronic, mechanical, photocopy, recording, or other–except for brief quotations in printed reviews, without prior permission of the author.

Paperback ISBN: 9798822964907

FINDING BALANCE POETRY

I'M NOT
NO SUPERWOMAN
AND I DON'T
CLAIM TO BE

MISS Q.

TABLE OF CONTENTS

Devils Intentions 1	Grief 31
The Other Woman 2	Fairytale 32
Heaven Gained an Angel 3	Priceless. 33
Chained 4	Sleepless Nights. 34
Repercussions. 5	If I was a Tool 35
Pieces of Me 6	Never Forget 36
Trying to Stay Afloat 7	My Writings on the Wall 38
Her and Not Me 8	Drama in the Workplace 40
Tornadoes. 9	Irritation 41
SUPERWOMAN. 10	Accordingly 43
Renewed 12	"How I became me" 45
My Angel 14	Calendars. 47
Mothers Comfort. 16	Create Your Own… 59
Confidence is my Virtue 17	Stay Organized 61
Foolish 18	Blank Canvas 73
HAVE A NICE LIFE. 20	Color Me!. 78
What's love got to do with it 22	Journal 100
The Power of Speech 23	Activities 102
Trapped In my Feelings 25	Laughter is good for the heart 113
I SEE RIGHT THROUGH YOU 28	Word Search Answer Keys 116
The Real Thing 29	

DEVILS INTENTIONS

I think moving forward is sometimes hard to see, progression becomes irrelevant when compared to what I need

Sometimes I feel as if I am moving in circles, and I just can't seem to jump over all these hurdles

I need to do this, I don't have time for that, I'm not trying to make excuses I am just merely stating facts

I just can't regain my focus, structure and order is what I lack, why can't this life of mine just cut me a little slack

My bodies breaking down from these big ole loads of stress, the weight of the world is on my shoulders, and I can feel it in my chest, and I just can't seem to find the time or patience for this mess

Please don't judge me, you don't know what I've been through, and I don't have time to listen to your one-sided point of view

I'm slowly sinking, and I just can't regain control, mind is racing, palms are sweating, and it just seems as if I can never be consoled, tears are flowing, chest is hurting, and I've reached an all-new type of low

Ok wait, let me think, please someone tell me what should I do? Devil bye, I ain't breaking, honey please don't misconstrue

Walking this road may get tough, and sometimes I may fall, sometimes I may stumble, and I might even have to crawl

I'll keep pushing, push right through it, you will never see me quit, not naïve, far from stupid, I understand your rhetoric. Wow, I feel better, I bet that wasn't your intent!!

Miss Q

Dedicated to my sister: GOD gives his biggest battles to his strongest warriors, and I see a warrior in you.

THE OTHER WOMAN

As I lay my head down, I can't help but to think I am better

But it is she that gets the real pleasure

The pleasure of knowing that he is truly hers, not just a mate for a moment in time

Not just someone he is with, but someone he loves

When he penetrates me, it feels like forbidden ecstasy?

My body yearns for his touch, even though I know he is not truly mines

But for that one night, I pretend to be, just as important as she, and when I awake, reality checks in, and I see, but I occur to still be blind

Blind to the fact, that he is a man, and his needs will be met by me for the time being, but it is she that holds his heart, and sooner than later our bodies will have to part

Later, in life he will forget about me, hopefully I will be a fond memory, one that makes him smile at the thought of me

In my mind, I stand second to none, but in his mind, she is first and foremost #1

I am his lover and a distant friend, as much as I don't want to say it I am merely just **The Other Woman!!**

Miss O

HEAVEN GAINED AN ANGEL

Heaven gained an Angel …. even through his struggles he always tried to smile, telling jokes and staying silent for awhile

Heaven gained an Angel, wipe away those tears my precious child

Hard times kept him humble, he didn't complain, nor did he question why

Heaven gained an Angel, joy cometh in the morning, don't you fret, oh please don't cry

Free is what they called him, spirit blowing through the wind

Heaven gained an Angel, I pray to one day meet again

Although his journey may have seemed short in length to us, it may have been traveled well spent

Heaven gained an Angel, there is only one other who knows the true burden of the distance

Heaven gained an Angel, Lets rejoice he is finally free from all this sin

Heaven gained an Angel; we don't know just where he's been!!!

Yes, we lost a husband, father, brother, uncle, and a friend, but we also gained an Angel to watch over us until our unexpected End!!!

Heaven Gained an Angel… Heaven Gained an Angel…Heaven Gained an Angel…. Amen

Miss Q

CHAINED

I want to break the chain of jealousy

I want to break the chain of lies

I want to provide truth for our future youth

I want to break the bond that ties

This bond ties us to ignorance

This bond ties us to wrong

We haven't even noticed, because we've been tied for so long

Let us do away with the hatred

Let us do away with the pain

Let us lift each other up, even if there is no personal gain

I want to break the chain of silence

I want to break the chain of blame

I want to push towards positivity, and there is no room for shame

Let us continue to encourage each other, stop pushing one another down

Let us fight for our progression; we have to do it now

Let us break the chain my people, don't let this cycle continue

Let us break the chain I know you have it in YOU!!!

FOOD FOR THOUGHT< HEART HEAVY

Miss Q

REPERCUSSIONS

If leaders tear down, the minority, it will eventually have a negative effect on the majority

Leaders must maintain a certain set of priorities

Anybody can possess money and fame, and it won't classify you as a leader, leaders lead by example not just by placing the blame

In order to accomplish greatness, a person must possess a certain level of patience

Leaders can't push out false allegations, and have absolutely no tact when making statements

Being rich doesn't give anyone the right to promote hate & violence, and then look to the same people that was disrespected for alliance or to be silent and in compliance

Back in the good ole days is where bad leadership will eventually take us, this is why certain communities and law enforcement can't seem to build trust

My question is this, what good ole days, let's take a minute and reminisce

Back when humans were classified as property, and they could be owned, bought, and sold accordingly

Or back when mutilating, beating, branding, lynching, and raping other human beings was legal, or maybe even when separate was disguised as equal

I pray to GOD no one is talking about those good ole days, because I highly doubt it would play out that way

We have come to far as a nation to keep letting hate and biases divide us, we are all a part of the human race, and when that casket drops it is ashes to ashes and dust to dust

I don't know about y'all, but I am just tired of all the commotion, but I promise you this, we have to go the right way, if we don't our economy will become stagnant, and the human race will remain broken

But anyways let me leave you with this, too many of our ancestors have paid the ultimate price for us as a people to be able to exercise our rights, for some of them this was their one and only dying wish

Miss Q

PIECES OF ME

Love has failed me

In my mind

I try to define the way

It is supposed to be,

But all I see is the abuse that has challenged me,

With the term, you call love

It has bruised me

Not physically, but mentally

It has disturbed my every being

And made me weak

In understanding the beautiful side that you see

My mind is shattered,

And my heart is broken

In relentless and wandering pieces of me!!!!!!!

TRYING TO STAY AFLOAT

Trying to keep my head above water sometimes

I get lost in the sea

Staying afloat is just not where my heart takes me

I am drowning in tears of sorrow, oh hear my plea

Rescue me from thoughts of affliction

Stop pointing and judging and take a moment out to listen

Listen to my screams as low as whispers

Look into my eyes at faded and far away pictures

Search into my soul as deep as any endless whole

Know that my dreams are better reflections of Gold, know that I did love once

But now I have shut my feelings and emotions out in the cold

Look at me like the waves of the sea, just flowing currents

Waiting for someone to have mercy on me!!

Miss Q

HER AND NOT ME

I sit and think about my past, about the good and the bad

Think about the relationships that did not last

There's only one that sticks in my mind, makes me want to ride a wave and go back in time

To the day when all I could think of was him

To the days when our so-called relationship came to an end

Sometimes I think I am crazy to have been in love with this evil human being

I just want to wake up from this nightmare I am constantly dreaming

Why do I love him? Why do I care?

Why do I love someone who will never be there?

He ended up loving someone else, and she is what I would call a friend

I try to get over it but there is still jealousy held deep within

Sometimes I want to throw up my hands and fight, knock the hell out of him and make him tell me why

Was it the color of my skin?

The length of my hair?

The frown on my face?

Maybe my sometimes-evil glare?

To make him fall for her and not me, and leave me to feel heartless and empty

It's been two years 3 days, and 2 nights, and my heart is healing, but I sit and wonder sometimes

Why she holds on to his heart and I hold on the love I have for him that just won't seem to die!!!!!

Miss Q

TORNADOES

Dreaming of a tornado that swept me up and was spinning me all around, and when it was done spinning it must've dropped me to the ground

I'm looking through the swirls and I see a whole bunch of white air, the wind just keeps twirling me, I feel so helpless with despair

I really don't know if I'm alive or if I'm dead, I can't even decipher if my feet are above my head

I think I'm crying tears, or is it precipitation from this big old spinning cloud, I must be screaming but the wind is howling loud

Please lord save me I want to be there for my kids, please provide me with your strength from up above, I want to be there for everyone I love

Wrap your arms around me and guide me from this storm, I need your grace and mercy please protect and make me warm

Can you hear me asking father can you hear my cries, Jesus please I don't think I am ready for my demise

The wind is getting is lighter, the spinning has suddenly stopped, the howling is at a distance and immediately I am dropped!!!

I'm looking all around me and I realize I am safe, and within seconds my eyes open to a bright and sunny day

Sometimes life reminds me of being caught in a tornado, situations you cannot control

Hectic schedules, all the judges, worldly riches, survival of the fittest, all this drama, sometimes always takes a toll

He never promised that storms would not come, but if he rests within you, then victorious you become

A little tornado is nothing to my GOD, he will quiet the winds, so that you will not hear a sound

He will stop the spinning, bring the twirling to an end, and bring you safely to the ground!!!

Miss Q

SUPERWOMAN

I ain't no superwoman, and I don't claim to be, but there is a superwoman within me!!!

Have I ever been mistreated and played just like a fool, failed at what I strived for, days and nights just filled with gloom

But did I bounce back with resilience showing strength, and shining bright, even with this disdainful world we live in my light could not be dimmed of all its brilliance

See I ain't no superwoman, and I don't claim to be, but there is a superwoman within me

Yes, I do face trials and tribulations, spiked emotions, sometimes lies, no set times, always running low on patience

Yes, I want to snap, but instead I just sit back, and let these so-called worldly enemies attack, trying my best to keep my sanity intact

So, let me say this again

I ain't no superwoman, and I don't claim to be, but there is a superwoman within me

See with each failed try, and with each time I want to throw up my hands, and drop to my knees, and ask my GOD why??

Just know it takes a super type of woman to look to the sky, and realize even JESUS was crucified

See super woman is supposed to know how to fly, but here on Earth that type of power can easily be denied, and I know I ain't no superwoman but these eyes of mine still look to the sky, and these invisible wings will continue to soar high

So please let me make this clear, I ain't no superwoman, and I don't claim to be, so I apologize on my behalf in advance for your insecurities, and I ask don't be angry with me when you see how confident I choose to be

Just know I don't claim to be no superwoman

Superwoman is just who evolved within me!!!

Miss O

RENEWED

I am writing this to the best man I have ever known

I asked GOD for a blessing of my very own,

It seemed impossible, because we live in a world where monogamy is rare, and hardly ever shown

I never knew there were men like you, I never believed, I didn't have a clue.

I was used to a world, where women were made of independence, and a man was hardly in attendance

My expectations were negative and my thoughts of relationships were skewed,

But because of you, my faith and hope in men will forever be renewed.

You stimulate me mentally, physically, and emotionally,

And I just have to express my love for you vocally and boastfully

Because I want you and everyone else to understand,

That you are the epitome of a great man

I don't think I ever knew what a father was supposed to do,

Until I had my very first child, and I thank GOD, every day that it was with you,

Three babies later and I think my love has stretched even further than I ever knew.

Because of you my confidence has grew,

And ladies if you listening that is what a real man is supposed to do.

He is supposed to build you up, not drag you down, and have you second guessing if he is going to stick around

I never feel like I'm in competition with other women, because he makes it known from the beginning

That I hold the keys to his heart, and his love for me is endless,

Anything involving other women would be downright senseless

All in all, I wouldn't be the woman I am today

Without you by my side, and I know sometimes I forget to say

 How lucky I am to have you in my life,

But just know I love you more than you will ever realize,

And you are forever more my ANGEL in disguise.

MY ANGEL

My man is honest, patient, and true

I don't feel the need to teach or tell him what to do

He makes me smile, even when I'm feeling low

My love for him is endless more than he will ever know

When I'm in doubt, and I need a listening ear

He is always around showing me that he cares

We have this chemistry that cannot be explained, and our passion for each other

Is so intense it drives me insane

When our lips touch it is more than just a kiss

I feel as if our souls interlock,

I've never felt anything like this

His attitude is amazing always positive and kind,

He makes it very clear that he is all mine

Yes we disagree, and we have our little fights,

But our arguments decease once the lights go out at night

I love his whole demeanor towards the goals he sets in life

I want to be his rock, his other half, and eventually his wife

I know I fuss him out and I'm irritating as well,

 But I am trying to show him better than I can tell

That I'm the one for him, this is more than just a fling,

God has blessed me with this man, this is the real thing

He is more than just my man; he is my gift from up above

He is the reflection of what God gives, and that is nothing but pure love

I prayed for all the pain to stop, no more tears no more lies

So, God decided to bless me with this Angel in disguise

Miss Q

Dedicated to the love of my life ♥

MOTHERS COMFORT

When I see them crying?

I hurt it is like the pain is just as deep as their wounds

My heart breaks with each tear that drops

The agony won't end until the pain that they might feel stops

When I see them try, I began to think of ways to prepare them for long and lonely days

I want them to be strong, but when they are weak I know their faith will help them carry on

I'll make sure to take the lead, and do anything I can to help them overcome the obstacles that's steps before their paths

And in the end, I know that they will come out victoriously and triumph over all the devil's tasks

When my spirit is lifted to those Heavenly gates, a piece of me will be with them, and even though I am dead and gone, a piece of me will be imbedded in their souls for the rest of their seasons, which will allow me to live on

My love for them is endless, they are gifts from GOD to me

And my amount of love for them is equally balanced with infinity

I remember the days when I doubted I would ever discover, the gift of being someone's mother

I am first and foremost their mother, and I hope to one day be a friend, because I will always be their comfort and confidant till the End!!!

Miss Q

CONFIDENCE IS MY VIRTUE

My confidence is a reflection of me

I don't shout about my inner and outer beauty

Because I know it is more than what the eye of the beholder might see

At times I am timid and shy

And at other I am out spoken and bold

Oh yes, I am definitely one of a kind

The makings of me are way more than I might show

But that is what makes my difference so bone chilling cold

You can't look at me and figure me out

But once you really see me you will always see what I'm about

The way I care for others has no limits

But don't take it as a weakness because my soul is slightly wicked

Don't come at me sideways, because the beast within me will be more than ready to escape

And put you in a choke hold that not even the devil his self can break

My words are like fire they will burn you till the tip of your soul

So, after I speak, I'll be your one and only desire

So, for everyone who wants to know who I am?

And what makes my spirit so strong

I am a queen in many virtues and forms

Miss Q

FOOLISH

She thought you were the one for her

She thought your love was true

She thought you would stay forever, once you both said I do

Never did she think that you would tell her lies

Never did she think that her man would be the cause of her cries

You say you want to leave before you cause her any pain

But the very thought of losing you is driving her insane

She thought you were a man that would stick by your word

Never did she think that you would have the nerve

To promise her a life filled with love and happiness

Then take back your promise, it just doesn't make any sense

She tried to fulfill your needs in every single way

But I guess it wasn't good enough, because you still don't want to stay

She still don't want to leave you, her love is very blind,

But believe it or not it shall happen in due time

You made this commitment under God, to cherish her as your wife

But now you're willing to let her go without even putting up a fight

You take her love for granted and you don't even see that what you have in her

No one else could ever be

One day in the future you shall realize that you made a big mistake

But hopefully by that time it will be too late

She thought you were the one for her

She thought your love was true

You're not what she thought you were

You're nothing but a fool!!!!

Miss Q

Dedicated to a friend, he ain't nothing but a fool girl

HAVE A NICE LIFE

Why did you decide to come back into my life if you were just going to cause havoc and strife?

You just had to pursue me into giving in cuz you knew if I gave in once that I would come again and again

Giving you a little of me piece by piece, trying so hard to fight the emotions that were stirring inside of me

Trying to push you away because I knew where it would lead, but in the end I failed and quickly gave in to all your needs

I knew there was another I saw it in your eyes, I should have listened to my first sense I keep asking myself WHY

I bet you get off on seeing me hurt; I can't even be mad because I should have followed my instincts and stayed more alert

You act like you don't care for me not even a little bit, like 8 months ago you weren't ready to drop everything and commit

Now you are saying it is her that you want, make up your mind, and stop wasting our time, because it seems to me that your love is oh so very blind

You probably just met this girl and already in love, already saying that she is the one

You don't know the true meaning

You don't know how to feel

To jump from me to her so easily, it all seems unreal

Or did you ever really feel the way you said you felt

Oh, I get it you must be playing a game of hearts, and those were the cards you were dealt

I'm so sick of being hurt I don't know what to do, my mind is all boggled and I'm so confused

I am going to be strong and just let you be, my heart will heal after time and once I set you free

I am going stay me and always stay true, I'm not going to change for anyone most definitely not you, I am really and truly through

I don't want to speak to you, don't even want you in my line of sight, I hope you and your new girl HAVE A NICE LIFE..........................

Miss O

This is not a poem that blames things on love, it is not love that causes you to hurt, but it is people that inflict pain on others, so just because one person hurts you doesn't mean give up on love all together, because there are good people out there, so I encourage everyone that reads this poem to keep looking for the real thing because it is out there!!!!!!!

WHAT'S LOVE GOT TO DO WITH IT

If I love you, why does it matter?

Will you change your demeanor towards me, and will we end up living together happily ever after

Will the arguments stop, is the fighting going to cease to exist

Will we end up a happy couple living in pure bliss

Do you promise not to hurt me, never make me cry?

And just because I am asking don't feel like you have to tell a lie

I want to say I do, but at the same time I don't, because in the end

What is it going to prove?

Nothing oh nothing, and in this battle my heart will still lose

You will be fine, because your mind will be set free contemplating your feeling for me

I'm not ready for love, my heart has not healed

From past relationships that were beaten and killed

Killed by promiscuity and dishonesty

Do I love you, I just can't say, do you love me why does it matter anyway, when you can't stay!!!!!!

Miss Q

P.s. Tina said it best

THE POWER OF SPEECH

Speak to me, speak to me, speak to me SPEAK

The sound of your voice is what my soul seeks

Don't act so quiet, I know you're not shy

When we converse, I get naturally high

I am a person who loves to conversate

Through words is how I deal with the world TODAY

I need to hear music like I need to hear you

Tell me about your day, and all the dreams you will pursue

Don't keep your feelings bottled in, just because you think I might perceive you as weak

All your secrets and fears I promise to keep

Speak to me, speak to me, speak to me, SPEAK

If we don't keep things from one another, let two become one

Just open your mouth and let the words run

Then I'll love shall grow to be more than complete

Let us not dismiss the POWER OF SPEECH

Speak to me, speak to me, speak to me, SPEAK

Let Day become night and night become day

Minutes to hours let's just talk them away

I know you're thinking who talks this much

But through words is how people are able to trust

Let me be the journal that only you may see

I won't reveal myself to anyone, even if they torture me

I need to hear your voice, thoughts, and opinions

That is why implore you to SPEAK

I want our love to grow stronger through speech

Speak to me, speak to me, speak to me, SPEAK!!!!!!!!!!

Miss Q

TRAPPED IN MY FEELINGS

Have you ever felt full

Not I ate too much full

But heart heavy full

Head clouded full

Tears won't stop flowing full

Have you ever felt weak

Not body aching weak

But not understanding weak

Scared to speak weak

Repeating the same mistakes weak

Have you ever felt tired

Not I'm sleepy tired

But too much going on tired

Lies over lies tired

Feeling like giving up tired

Have you ever felt proud

Not you did a good job proud

But I am too proud to beg proud

I don't want it but I need it proud

Stubborn to the core proud

Have you ever felt beaten

Not physically abused beaten

But literally kicked when your already down beaten

See you at the finish line beaten

Don't even want to try anymore beaten

Have you ever just wanted to

Lie down and never get up

Not actually die, but not actually live

Not wanting to walk because the process

Of crawling before you walk

Frightens your very thoughts

I just want to feel free

Let me out this cage free

Release me from these mental chains free

The sky is the limit free

Take these feelings lock them in a box

Throw away the key free

This is how it feels to be me!!!!!!!!!!!!!!!!!!!!!!!

Miss Q

I SEE RIGHT THROUGH YOU

When you look into my eyes, do you really see me

Can you read my thoughts of despise, do you see what I aspire to be

Or can you not see past my facial expression, as I stand there with seriousness written all over my face

Just waiting for you to think about my skin selection, wondering if you even notice your own stares of hate

You tell others that you respect me, and that you will treat me as an equal, but deep in your soul, you and I both know different

Instead, you hide your thoughts knowing that your truth can be lethal

So, you smile in my face with fake eyes and fake thoughts, even tricking yourself into believing you are not at all concerned with race

I try to be positive and not think that all is lost, but my eyes seek the truth, even if it reeks of filth and waste

You want me to trust and listen to you, and put my life in your hands

And if I choose to go against you, you don't forget to hit me with the proper reprimands

I sit back and watch your interaction with others, I see how you let their behavior slide on by, Even a blind man would have to sit and wonder

Where your true feelings lye

Whatever is done in the dark shall come to light, and when it does, I'll be there ready for that fight

Miss Q

THE REAL THING

I am sick of settling for less

I'm not looking for a fairy tale

Just looking for my heart to be relieved of this stress

Searching for that moment in time where I can exhale knowing that what I

 Share with another is real

I want to be able to wake up in the morning and, know that the relationship I have is ideal

Not based on lies and dishonesty but based on truth and companionship

Always keeping loyalty, and never placing doubt on the relationship

I am hoping for a real love

The kind of love God intended for woman and man to share

One that I can be proud of

 A love that has no heartache or despair

Being able to stay faithful, not running to another's bed because of an argument, or something he said

Knowing that as our hearts intertwine

Our souls shall become one and with that we shall shine brighter than the moon and the sun

I'm through with failed relationships and useless little flings

I'm searching for passion and true love

I am ready for the real thing!!!!!!!!!!!!

Miss Q

Inspired by: A friend, you deserve the real thing!

GRIEF

See at first it was really painful for me to witness death suddenly surrounding you see

No more talks and intimate conversations, smiles are lost, and tears dwell in preservation

Didn't want to see the onset of tears form in their eyes,

Couldn't bare for them to ask, and didn't even know a reason 'Why'

How can I help, what can I do, show me how I can be of support for you?

My mouth is speaking, my mind is thinking, my heart is beating, all the while my emotions are steadily sinking

Before I know it, I've lost control, and somehow, I'm now the one who needs to be consoled

I think to myself what's wrong with me, emotional regulation is nowhere within my reach

Suck it up, get it together, this is not the time for you to display your vulnerabilities

Someone needs you, be a support, be a friend, this is not the time for you to try and lean on them

I now look at death through a lens of fallacy and by doing this I am able to reject my wayward empathy

Yes, I still cringe at the thought of loved ones in emotional agony, however now when I witness death so suddenly, unexpectedly,

I equate death with being 'Free'

Miss O

P.S. How do you help a person that is grieving? Have you grieved all your losses? What is true empathy? Why did Jesus Weep? These all questions that I ask myself.

FAIRYTALE

I want the fairytale

I want that white picket fence, the barbecues, and family vacations

Let me make this make sense, I want the honey I dos and the family relations

See I want the Fairytale

Please just cuddle me close, kissing my forehead

While whispering sweet nothings, telling me I'm the one you love the most

Give me the fairytale

Intimate conversations last deep into the night

Nothing more than cuddling and holding, while reassuring me everything will be alright

I want the fairytale

I want the big house with love and laughter revolving in it, understanding there will be petty fights, and senseless arguments,

Still knowing nothing could be better than our overall commitment

I sit in wonder

Can I make this fairytale existent……….

Miss Q

May 8, 2008
PRICELESS

Did you know that this candy is priceless?

Worth more than any value you put on your wish list

No, Santa definitely won't be delivering this

And please don't ask whose is it, if I ever decide to let you taste this

The only reason I am letting you get a taste, is because just like an addict

My candy provides a fix, and when you feel the need to get high

Your heart will start to race, like you have just been kicked

Don't ask what the price is because it is not for sale

Until something real can come along and break the spell

It is worth more than you can ever imagine, more than what is in your bank accounts

More than clothes and fashion, more than any type of thrills

More than you would like to admit, and more than any lies you will submit

Don't front like you don't know who runs the show

Did you know this candy is priceless, well now you know!!!!!!!!!

Miss Q

SLEEPLESS NIGHTS

At first, I couldn't sleep without him

Now I am content to the point where

I lay in the bed

And as time goes by the thought of

His touch lingers through my head, after about an hour two

I am on a magic carpet ride

Dreaming and wishing he is right there by my side

Images of the love we had that wouldn't prevail haunting my dreams

I awaken staring at the blank ceiling

Thinking about a love that time would stand still for

Thinking about a love that has no end

With all the heartache that I have endured

I still have hope for a love so pure

If loving him is wrong, damn I don't want to be right

But maybe just maybe when time has healed my wounds

A real love will come into my life

Until then I am content with just dreaming about him being by my side!!!!!!!!!!

Miss Q

IF I WAS A TOOL

If I was a hoe the things I would do

I'd make you my slave and I'd be yours too

If I was a tool, I'd say forget the mind

Just give me the work, let's not waste any time

If you were a prospect that I'd like to fix

I'd tell you the real deal and you would follow the script

No beating around the bush no playing any games,

Just getting to work it helping you maintain

Maintaining the work, constantly putting out fires

Giving you help, so your body won't tire

If I was a tool, it'd be just one night

No kissing, no holding, no pointless fights

No baby I love you, no domestic abuse

Just get the job done and then cut me loose

It'd be done and over, I'd go to the next repeating old history, settling for less

If I was a tool I'd lack respect, for my mind or my body

I'd wouldn't have to utilize intellect

Being a tool is something I do not wish to become, this I can guarantee

Ask yourself this question so you will see what I mean

If you were a tool, how might you be????????

Miss Q

Dedicated to: A friend

NEVER FORGET

I've seen sunsets through purple and pinkish skies

I've heard stories told of my sweet ancestor's demise

I've never been beaten, nor have I been sold

but the past of my people is etched in my soul

I'll never forget of all the sweat blood and tears

the struggle and weight they had to carry for years

They carried the weight of America right on their backs

through each generation, the hope of freedom still intact

stolen and captured from foreign land

shackled and chained by what they knew as the white man

mistreated and enslaved because of their race

mothers and daughter subjected to rape

never giving up, hearts filled with strife

killed for no reason, hate in their eyes

using our own to capture one another,

oh, how they tried to break down the strong black brotha

to look a white man or woman straight in the eye was known as a crime

To be beaten and hung from a tree was their punishment back in that time

segregated schools to the back of the bus is what they were told was a must

still, they stood strong with white picket signs, protest and rallies

thoughts of equality in the back of their minds

yes, change has come over the years,

but I'll shall always remember their pain and despair

shades of purple and pink form in the sky

and I think of the past that my people survived

day after day with each sunset

those memories are something I'll shall never forget

Miss O

P.S. A lil something for black history month hope you enjoy

02-2018

MY WRITINGS ON THE WALL

Song Verse "Back in the day when I was young I'm not a kid anymore, but some days"

I sit and wonder, because some of my thoughts of me can make me feel so small

Certain days I sit and wish I was a kid again, while on others I cringe at the thought

My writings on the wall

Today I realized that I am a hopeless romantic

That will never experience the lifestyle with that

White picket fence, no fairytale for me, no utopian happy ending,

Just the plain ole ordinary

My writings on the wall

Just because they thought I was expendable,

Doesn't mean I should, telling yourself what to feel can easily be misunderstood

You tell your mind one thing, but your heart feels another, it then becomes a battle and I am left to suffer

My writings on the wall

That day I felt victorious, this day I feel unfortunate

I got the devil on one shoulder, and an angel on the other

And they are in a full-blown argument, acting like sister and brother

Song Verse "The Light" By: Common "There are times when you need someone I will be by your side wellll"

My Writing on the Wall

Who in the flesh is actually there when you need them?

Some people can't even be there for themselves in this life forms

So ready to condemn, and they are the cause of most signs of mayhem

Already conformed, our thought process has become the basic norm

My writings on the wall

Sometimes I feel as though it's just too much too bare

Even though I know I'm blessed beyond compare

I seek wisdom through his words, he speaks to me verse after verse

My writings on the wall

And do you know what GOD said to me

Pain is a blessing in the, when you feel pain, you know that you are free

And your eyes are open to see, that is when you finally seek comfort in me

My writings on the wall

Written for everyone to see

No need to search my eyes for a story

My writings on the wall bares my truth openly

A fly would have no Glory

Miss Q

05-2017

DRAMA IN THE WORKPLACE

There's too much drama at the workplace, so much hate just stirring around

Lots of glaring, no one caring, just keep quiet don't make a sound

Too much drama at the workplace, talking bad behind your backs

What's she wearing, no information sharing, and I just can't get down with that

No one leading by example, quick to throw you under the bus

Petty people always trying to make a fuss

When did work become so hostile?

What happened to activities and task being complete?

And by doing this a person gains a certain livelihood and self esteem

I thought work consisted of sustaining, building, and growing in all aspects in life

All I see is bickering and complaining, too much drama, too much strife

Too much drama at the workplace, I see why our economy is in decline

We think the work is the problem, we think people are being lazy, maybe we think people just don't have the time

I think I beg to differ, just using personal experience, not being able to deal with difference

Makes it hard for a person to be gregarious

There is just too much drama at the workplace, too much competition, which takes a toll on the overall mission, no one wants to listen which causes opposition

What happened to compromise, instead all I see is the next person being patronized

Too much drama at the workplace, people don't respect themselves, which makes it hard for them to respect the next, no wonder all these negative effects

All this drama in the workplace, in the future we need to try and prevent, all this drama in the workplace just isn't time well spent!!!

Miss Q

IRRITATION

Oh, why oh why do you irritate me (song)

Oh, why oh why could it be? (song)

I mean from the constant reminders that people ain't it

Down to my soreness of breast, and cramps in my back when Auntie Flow comes to visit!

I mean isn't it enough to know that when it rains it pours, and

Although death doesn't come in fours, it still comes in threes

Which still in most case can be hard to conceive?

You continuously patronize me, irritation oh please leave me be

I'm already aware of misery being evident in daily activities, and

Yes, I know how he craves his company

Oh, why Oh why do you do this to me?

I hate how you pick on me day after day

My patience is on a constant decline, I'm picking my brain

I swear sometimes I think I'm going insane

I really need my own peace of mind

Jealousy plagues me, insecurities consummate me, and

Irritation you're the underlying factor of all of thee

I'm emotionally constipated, physically and mentally exasperated, and

Above all, I am just down right irritated.

Irritation, please just stay away from me!!!!

Miss Q

42

ACCORDINGLY

In this poem I want to talk about the other woman

Admittingly I've actually held that title a time or two

Not boasting or bragging, I'm just saying be careful

What you do, because you never know what damage

You may cause, until you have to walk in the other person's shoes

See from my constructed point of view, I was, and am the number one, and the number two,

And I hate to admit, but I might even be a fool, because somehow my man allowed for YOU another

Woman to stroke his ego, with impure residue, and instead of doing what I feel I ought to do

I AM going to attempt and try and speak life unto you, honey please don't let him, them, the world devalue you

I admit at first I just wanted to break you in two, pull out that weave and spit all over you,

The lowest act I could possibly do, I just wanted you to feel how I felt, but then I realized

You must be insecure to allow a couple of text and some words make you melt, and oh NO it

Wasn't your fault he didn't value his commitment when he said his I dos, but I will unapologetically push right on through

See I carried his seeds, and gave beautiful life unto thee, and even though I might hate what he has done to me

I still have an ultimate responsibility to love, protect, and carry on his legacy

So be it for richer or poorer, sickness, and in health till death do us part, at this point I am going to allow him to continue to hold the keys to my heart.

Please stop giving your body to someone who knows damn well they ultimately have nothing to offer you

He wasn't your friend, most definitely was not your man, he didn't even give a damn, not for you, not for me,

His vision was cloudy, what in the hell ever happened to monogamy, damn you got kids, stop putting out this ideology

That sleeping around is cool, and breaking up families is the thing to do

And yeah I know it should start with him, yes my husband will have to answer for this sin

But you are not the ultimate victim, neither am I, see honey, this type of situation goes way deeper than you and I

We have to dig up the roots of this here tree, look all the way through history, and take a peek at our ancestry, then really view our own community, then finally please try and examine your own family, and tell me what you see.

Another father absentee, one more divorcee, see stereotypically the other woman was and still is ME,

So please listen carefully, instead of trying to hurt you I want you to see that a QUEEN wears her crown accordingly.

Miss Q

P.S. Accordingly meaning: In a way that is appropriate to the particular circumstances. You can't call yourself a Queen if you out here doing this that and the other, so if you want to hold the title as a Queen act like one, and stop undermining your own worth.

"HOW I BECAME ME"

Starting with procreation, marked the beginning of my interesting journey

My parents were young in fact I believe my biological mom had just reached the age seventeen

Was love involved? I'm not quite sure, but there had to be some type of attraction, that just could not be ignored

Because about 9 months later I came to be, and at birth I was already labeled by society

Due to my specific anatomy, my first coined term, was girl, which would ultimately shape bits & pieces of my personality

And then there was the term African American, or black, which was given to me, in representation of my origin, culture, and last but not least, the color of my skin, one of the best parts of me

But little did I know that theses labels would be used to try and hold me back, little did I know these labels would also aid in macro & micro aggressive attacks

We all know that babies have no idea really about how life will turn out to be, I was just innocent & ignorant of all the experiences that would eventually shape how I became me

Skipping ahead a couple of years, I became familiar with how it felt to care, as well as how easy it was to fear

I eventually embarked on my early childhood, which on my part was dramatically misunderstood

Brown skin, pigtails, dirt & snot, nappy headed, boys with cooties, oh how easily I forgot

Riding bikes, street lights on, oh you're a girl you don't know how to fight

Baby dolls, playing house, close your legs you have on a skirt, I am still confused about what was actually wrong and what was actually right

Then came my middle years, when life revolved around all of my peers, so many silent tears, repressed showing exactly what I really feared., what were they wearing, what did they think, what were they saying, forget everyone else, all that mattered was that we were in sync

Looking back, I realize how naïve one could be, because oh how society shaped how I became me

Adolescence proved to be the hardest of all, hormones swayed my mood, sometimes I felt fine, while other times I felt oh so very small

The confusion was real, what happened to boys having cooties, I just didn't know how to feel

All I know is that when he would approach, my heart would start pounding and my tongue would be caught in my throat

Even worse lying in bed at night, thinking of him parts of me would start throbbing, what in the hell was wrong with me, right

I felt as if I was back to square one, just ignorant, confused, misunderstood, just wanted to be left alone by everyone

I just didn't see how this stage of my life would be important to the evolution of me

Early adulthood proved to be better, I was past first moments, and I actually was experiencing a lot more pleasure

I had found a new confidence, I believed me to be a hot commodity, due to specific qualities that were once frowned upon, in simplistic terms it was as if the duck had become the swan

Because I'm a girl I'm not supposed to fight, which brings me to my other term "Soldier" what an oversight, see all of these labels have developed me and how I walk through life, my experiences are representative of my intersectionality

I cannot be summed up by one specific term, label, and/ or category, mother, friend, soldier, daughter, lover, wife, the list can go on and on. It would take a lot more than just a poem to describe the makings of me!!!!!!

Miss Q

CALENDARS

JANUARY   YEAR: _____

Sunday	Monday	Tuesday	Wednesday	Thursday	Friday	Saturday
Today is Good!	I Got this!	I am enough!	I won't stop!	I am powerful!	Greatness is mine!	I am strong!
Challenges come!	I will be victorious!	Pain is growth!	Learn and grow!	Stay focused!	I am good!	I am ok!
Life produces Lessons!	I'm capable!	I'm resilient!	I am unique!	Gracious!	I'm beautiful!	Creative Thinking!
Thankful!	Think first!	Breath In!	Breath out!	Exhaling!	Energized!	Not worried!
Make it count!	Adventure!	Future moves!	Greatness!	I count!	Persistence Pays!	My best is great!
Persevere!	Practice control!	Standards produce!	Stop distractions!	Self-Care!	Self-Love!	Find Balance!

FEBRUARY

YEAR: _____

Sunday	Monday	Tuesday	Wednesday	Thursday	Friday	Saturday
Life happens!	Pain comes!	Keep pushing!	Don't give up!	Love Life!	Adversity strengthens	Diversity thrives!
Produce results!	Plan ahead!	I'm Here!	Take time!	Relax!	Sing!	Positive moods!
Change is ok!	I love me!	Make goals!	Say thank you!	Say Hello!	Speak up!	Keep trying!
Show heart!	Be courageous!	Joy Cometh!	Blow Bubbles!	Believe it!	Achieve it!	He lost!
He found!	Do it!	Visualize greatness!	Eat Healthy!	Call a friend!	Give yourself mercy!	Perfection is skewed!
Live!!	Plant seeds!	Succeed!	Forgive!	Be Bold!	Have fun!	Find Balance!

MARCH   YEAR: _____

Sunday	Monday	Tuesday	Wednesday	Thursday	Friday	Saturday
Reach out!	I am calm!	I am thoughtful!	I deserve…	I am able!	Seek counsel!	I inspire!
History teaches!	Trust!	Give!	I radiate!	I am powerful!	I matter!	My body is my temple!
I am grateful!	Show kindness!	Smile!	Read!	Write!	Set boundaries!	Be silly!
Vacation!	Spend time!	Expect the unexpected!	Take a class!	Exercise!	Its ok to cry!	Set routines!
Prioritize!	Creative positive habits!	Be safe!	I am kind!	I am valuable!	Show respect!	I am valid!
I have skills!	Think positive!	Ask for help!	Slow down!	Find solutions!	Love what you do!	Find Balance!

APRIL

YEAR: _____

Sunday	Monday	Tuesday	Wednesday	Thursday	Friday	Saturday
I ain't sorry!	Be better!	Work hard!	I am Phenomenal!	Create peace!	I have control!	Choose love!
Drink water!	Difference is better!	Laugh out loud!	Be free!	Simplicity!	Self-knowledge!	Inner wisdom!
No Conformity!	Invest!	Take a chance!	Stand out!	Values!	Ask a question!	Promote self!
Keep up!	Think outside the box!	You can!	Financially educate!	Deviate!	Ask why!	Overcome!
Establish foundation!	Expand!	Change Liabilities!	Think on your feet!	Create Assets!	Build Capitol!	I am sophisticated!
Reinvest!	I am rich!	Say No!	Say Yes!	Stop negativity!	Be Yourself!	Find Balance!

MAY   YEAR: _____

Sunday	Monday	Tuesday	Wednesday	Thursday	Friday	Saturday
I am strong!	Pay yourself!	Hard work!	I am ready!	Efforts help!	Succeed!	Make a real difference!
I am happy to be me!	I am grateful!	Goals are achievable!	I am confident!	Self-kindness!	I will practice!	Right paths!
I will act!	Success is mine!	Good in all things!	Always learning!	I trust myself!	Try new things!	I am safe!
I love myself!	Life is beautiful!	I am powerful!	I believe in…	It's ok!	Possibilities are endless!	Well-rested!
Full of energy!	I am relaxed!	I am strong in mind!	I am strong in body!	I am strong in spirit!	life is a gift!	I deserve love!
I deserve happiness!	I care for myself!	Fuel my body!	I will succeed!	I give myself!	Room to grow!	Find Balance!

JUNE YEAR: _____

Sunday	Monday	Tuesday	Wednesday	Thursday	Friday	Saturday
I can do this!	I feel great!	I'm so smart!	Like my life!	dreams come true!	I enjoy!	Good things!
I'm doing great!	This is a snap!	I am fine!	In charge!	Not worried!	Nobody like me!	Trust myself!
I'm focused!	I'm so lucky!	I'm amazing!	Good choices!	I'm a successful!	Welcome every day!	A better place!
Beautiful day!	One step at a time!	I love a challenge!	Good decisions!	I'm good!	Life is….	I'm unstoppable!
Bring it on!	I'm capable!	I'm exceptional	Great ideas!	What I do!	Every day counts!	Never give up!
Full of surprises!	Original!	I'm unique!	Whatever comes up!	Very talented!	Forward!	Find balance!

JULY

YEAR: _____

Sunday	Monday	Tuesday	Wednesday	Thursday	Friday	Saturday
Challenges are interesting!	We're all in!	Work out well!	I keep calm!	Carry on!	stay on track!	Persistence pays!
I persevere!	Earn new things!	I'm a positive!	I always give!	My best!	I don't worry!	What's important!
Business!	New opportunity!	Never overwhelmed!	Move on!	The next thing!	Fun every day!	Open mind!
Find my life!	Move toward what matters!	Guard my peace!	Cherish myself!	Here and now!	Don't get distracted!	High standards!
I learn from…	Finish what I start!	I'm a useful!	Don't waste time!	Take my time!	The best day!	I choose!
Good mood!	Have a positive attitude!	My reality!	Expect the best!	Eventually!	Becomes real!	Find Balance!

AUGUST

YEAR: _____

Sunday	Monday	Tuesday	Wednesday	Thursday	Friday	Saturday
Welcome change!	Welcome the unexpected!	Eager for…	Have what it takes!	Delighted with life!	Life is satisfying!	Interested in life!
Open to possibilities!	Welcome challenges!	I can accomplish!	Put my heart into!	I am joyful!	Because I am here!	Everything I need!
Love my work!	Keep growing!	Make my life happen!	Change every day!	Love succeeding!	Make a difference!	Deserve happiness!
Love myself!	Keep going!	Worth it!	I'm bubbling!	Attitude makes me thrive!	I am bold!	Value my ability!
My time!	Endless!	Make my life happy!	Everything I do!	Bright future!	Seize my chances!	Peacefully happy!
Keep my own counsel!	Delighted and surprised!	I know!	I inspire!	Confidence in others!	History of success!	Find Balance!

SEPTEMBER   YEAR: _____

Sunday	Monday	Tuesday	Wednesday	Thursday	Friday	Saturday
Scribble on paper!	Be with people!	Watch a comedy!	Hydrate!	Go see a movie!	Do a word search!	Do a crossword!
Do s choolwork!	All the good things!	Play a musical instrument!	Life is full!	Look at yourself!	Paint your nails!	Do your make-up!
Do your hair!	Sing!	Figure out a solution!	I can always….	Study the sky!	Punch a pillow!	Cover yourself!
Let yourself cry!	Take a nap!	Take a hot shower!	Choose good friends!	Earn trust!	Step away!	Take a hot bath!
Play with a pet!	Go shopping!	Have a warm heart!	Clean something!	I am proud of who!	Mind is sharp!	Knit or sew!
Read a good book!	Listen to music!	Aromatherapy!	Meditate!	Go somewhere!	Bake cookies!	Find Balance!

OCTOBER　　YEAR: _____

Sunday	Monday	Tuesday	Wednesday	Thursday	Friday	Saturday
Create a vision board!	Paint or draw!	Rip paper into pieces!	Shoot hoops!	Hug a pillow!	Hug stuffed animal!	Talk to someone!
Kick a ball!	Write a letter!	Send an email!	Plan your dream room!	Hyper focus!	Dance!	"Shop" online!
Make hot chocolate!	Play with modeling!	Build a pillow fort!	Take a long drive!	Complete something!	Build something!	Color-coordinate!
Draw on yourself!	Find a new hobby!	Look up recipes!	Cook a meal!	Visit a friend's house!	Talk to an older person!	Watch fish!
Go outside!	Pray!	List blessings!	Read the Bible!	Jump!	Contact a hotline!	Make a playlist!
Ride a bicycle!	Feed the ducks!	Color!	Memorize a poem!	Stretch!	Search for ridiculous things!	Find Balance!

NOVEMBER   YEAR: _____

Sunday	Monday	Tuesday	Wednesday	Thursday	Friday	Saturday
Play a 15-minute game!	Plan your wedding!	Plant some seeds!	Perfect your space!	Be wild!	Seek sunshine!	Be the reason!
Edit your pictures!	Play with a balloon!	Do a facial!	Play with childhood toys!	Collect something!	Make it happen!	You matter!
I love you because…	Play video!	Clean up trash!	Visit Local park!	Text or call a friend!	Know your worth!	Do good!
Rearrange furniture!	Look up new words!	Smile at five people!	Teach your pet!	Random act of kindness!	Things will work out!	Positive mindset!
Learn a new language!	Play with a child!	Go for a walk!	Put a puzzle together!	Clean your room!	Make a list of goals!	Follow your heart!
Hug a friend!	Move EVERYTHING!	Get together with friends!	Yoga!	Try to do handstands!	Search online!	Find balance!

DECEMBER   YEAR: _____

Sunday	Monday	Tuesday	Wednesday	Thursday	Friday	Saturday
Make sense!	Patience is power!	Stay hopeful!	Go Home!	Work in progress!	Be your own hero!	New adventures!
Protect peace!	Little things!	No Drama!	Escape!	Be still!	Everything connects!	Make a home run!
Walk away!	Run a marathon!	Climb!	Lift yourself up!	Lift up someone else!	Impressed!	No Limitations!
Avoid criticism!	Dare to fail!	Boldness has genius!	Easily forgive!	Never forget!	time is limited!	Use what you have!
Make a decision!	Go confidently!	Best time is now!	Everything has beauty!	Be of value!	No excuses!	Get to the point!
Regret nothing!	Tell the truth!	I'm sophisticated!	Emotionally regulate!	Control your life!	Right choices reflect hopes!	Find Balance!

CREATE YOUR OWN...

CREATE A SELF-AFFIRMING NAME POEM

Finding Balance through the creation of self-affirming poetry utilizing the letters in your name to list attributions that show positive self-reflection that flow together fluently.

Example: The name **Amy**

A is for Amazing delight

M is for Magnifying my light

Y is for Yummy but please don't bite

Name Poem

STAY ORGANIZED

Creating a checklist can help with organization and procrastination which declines stress levels

Self-Care	o Pray o Get Dressed o Drink Water o Go outside o Socialize o Exercise o Practice thankfulness o Eat Healthy o Learn something new o Take Mental Breaks o Give yourself mercy o Journal o Reflect
Home	o Clean i.e. (wash dishes, vacuum, wash clothes sweep, disinfect etc.) o Cook o Check equipment serviceability (i.e. HVAC, Water Heater, Garbage disposal etc. o Decorate o Grocery Shop o Utilize Space o Save money o Maintain outside areas o Inspect for insect invasion o Clean Vents o Check Security System o Replace non-serviceable items o Enjoy your space

Business	o Check Emails
	o Attend Meetings
	o Research
	o Complete daily assigned task
	o Take mental breaks
	o Be Professional
	o Be on time
	o Show respect
	o Set Boundaries
	o Ask Questions
	o Communicate Effectively
	o Delegate Appropriately
	o Stay Motivated

STAY ORGANIZED
Create Your Own Checklist

1.	
2.	
3.	
4.	
5.	
6.	
7.	
8.	
9.	
10.	

STAY ORGANIZED
Create Your Own Checklist

1.	
2.	
3.	
4.	
5.	
6.	
7.	
8.	
9.	
10.	

STAY ORGANIZED
Create Your Own Checklist

1.	
2.	
3.	
4.	
5.	
6.	
7.	
8.	
9.	
10.	

STAY ORGANIZED
Create Your Own Checklist

1.	
2.	
3.	
4.	
5.	
6.	
7.	
8.	
9.	
10.	

STAY ORGANIZED
Create Your Own Checklist

1.	
2.	
3.	
4.	
5.	
6.	
7.	
8.	
9.	
10.	

STAY ORGANIZED
Create Your Own Checklist

1.	
2.	
3.	
4.	
5.	
6.	
7.	
8.	
9.	
10.	

STAY ORGANIZED
Create Your Own Checklist

1.	
2.	
3.	
4.	
5.	
6.	
7.	
8.	
9.	
10.	

STAY ORGANIZED
Create Your Own Checklist

1.	
2.	
3.	
4.	
5.	
6.	
7.	
8.	
9.	
10.	

STAY ORGANIZED
Create Your Own Checklist

1.	
2.	
3.	
4.	
5.	
6.	
7.	
8.	
9.	
10.	

STAY ORGANIZED
Create Your Own Checklist

1.	
2.	
3.	
4.	
5.	
6.	
7.	
8.	
9.	
10.	

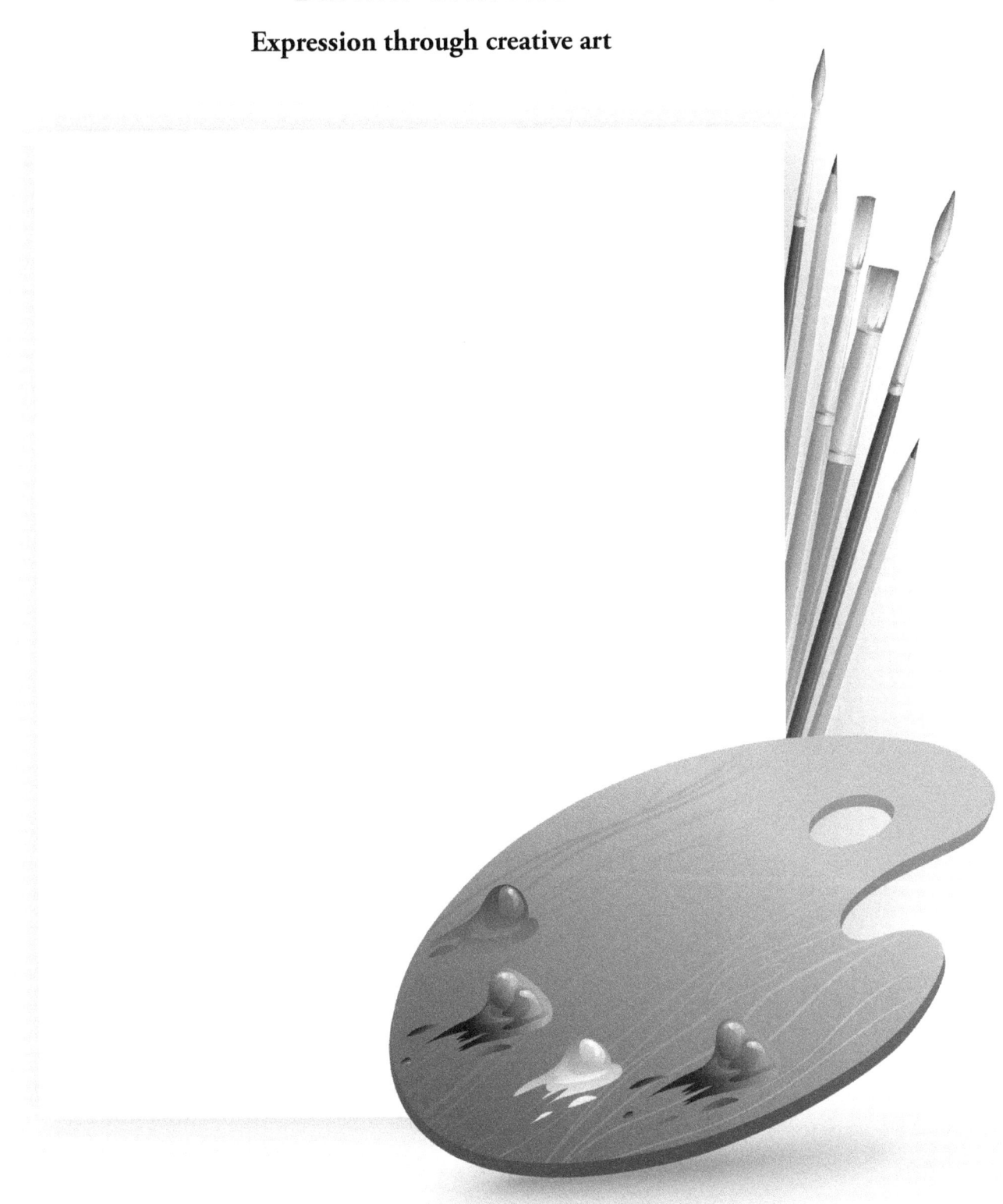

BLANK CANVAS
Expression through creative art

BLANK CANVAS
Expression through creative art

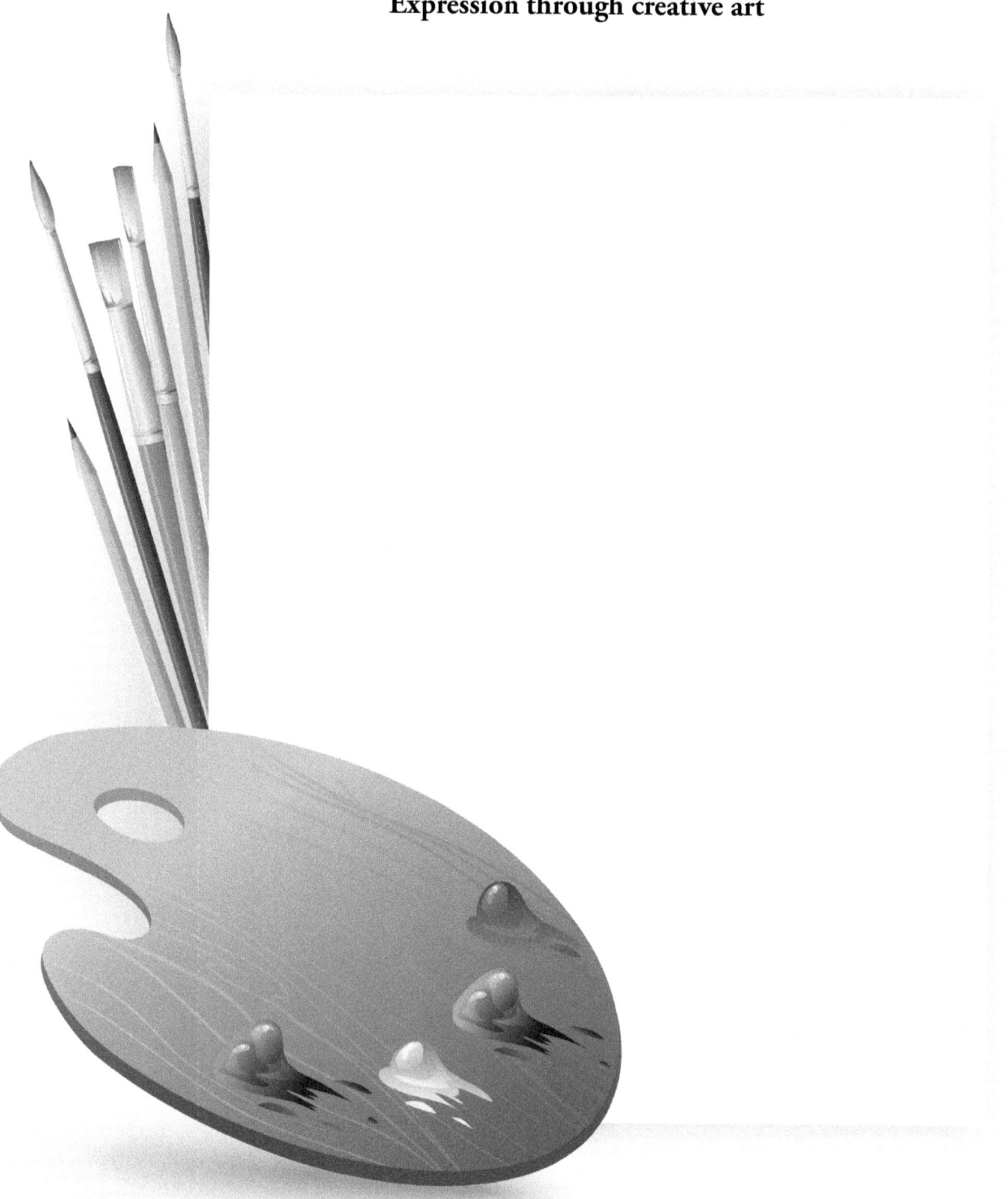

BLANK CANVAS
Expression through creative art

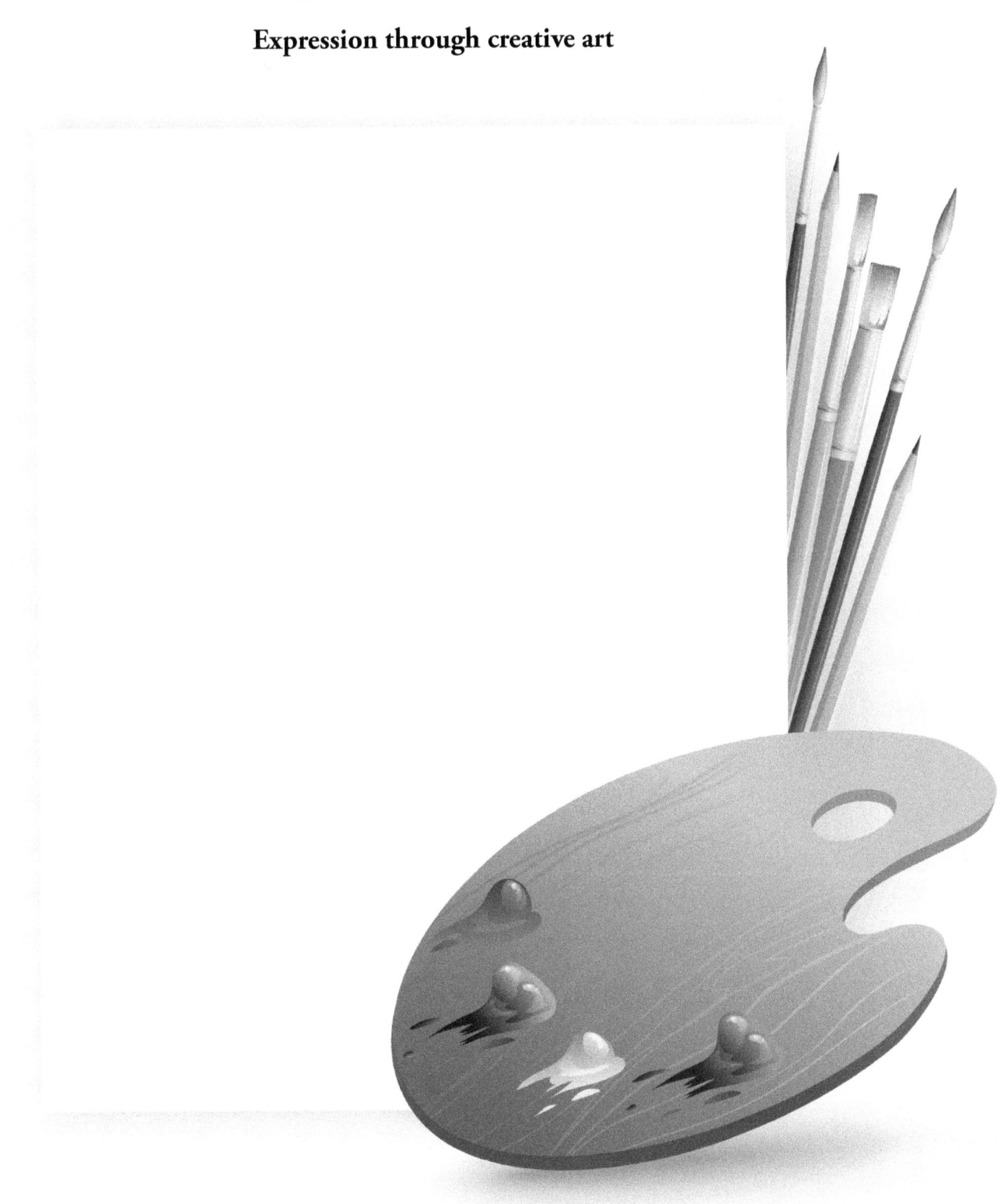

BLANK CANVAS

Expression through creative art

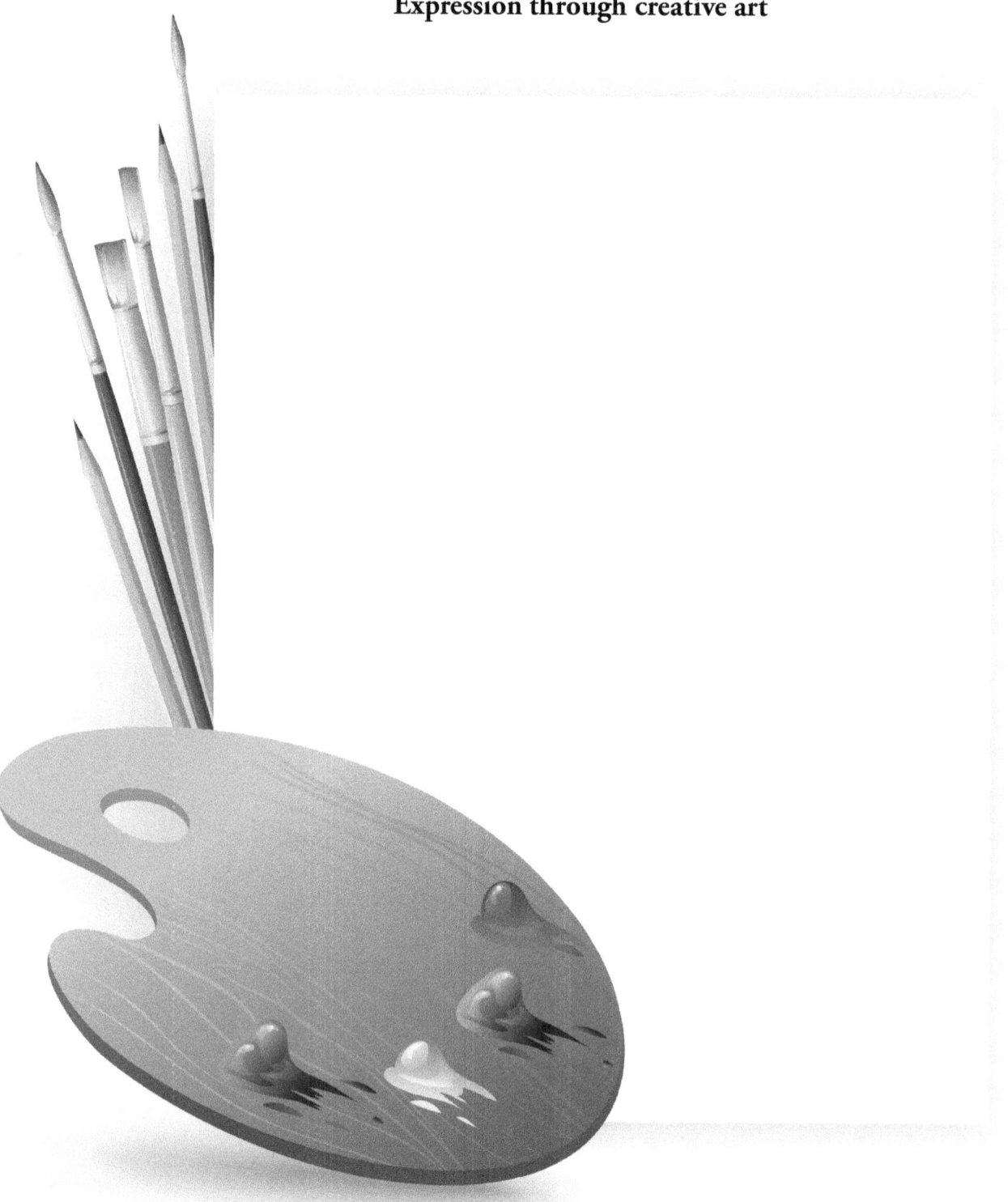

BLANK CANVAS
Expression through creative art

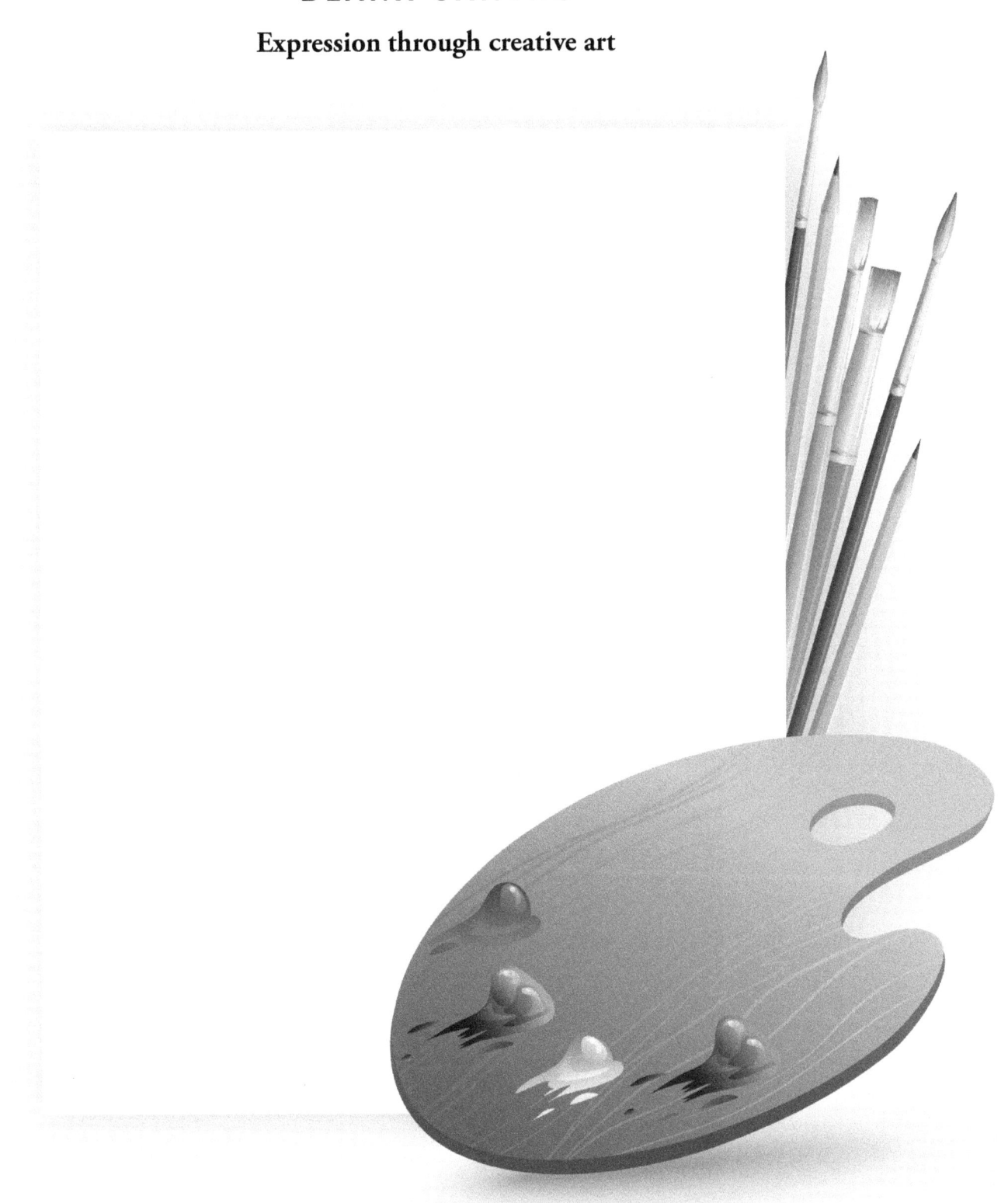

COLOR ME!

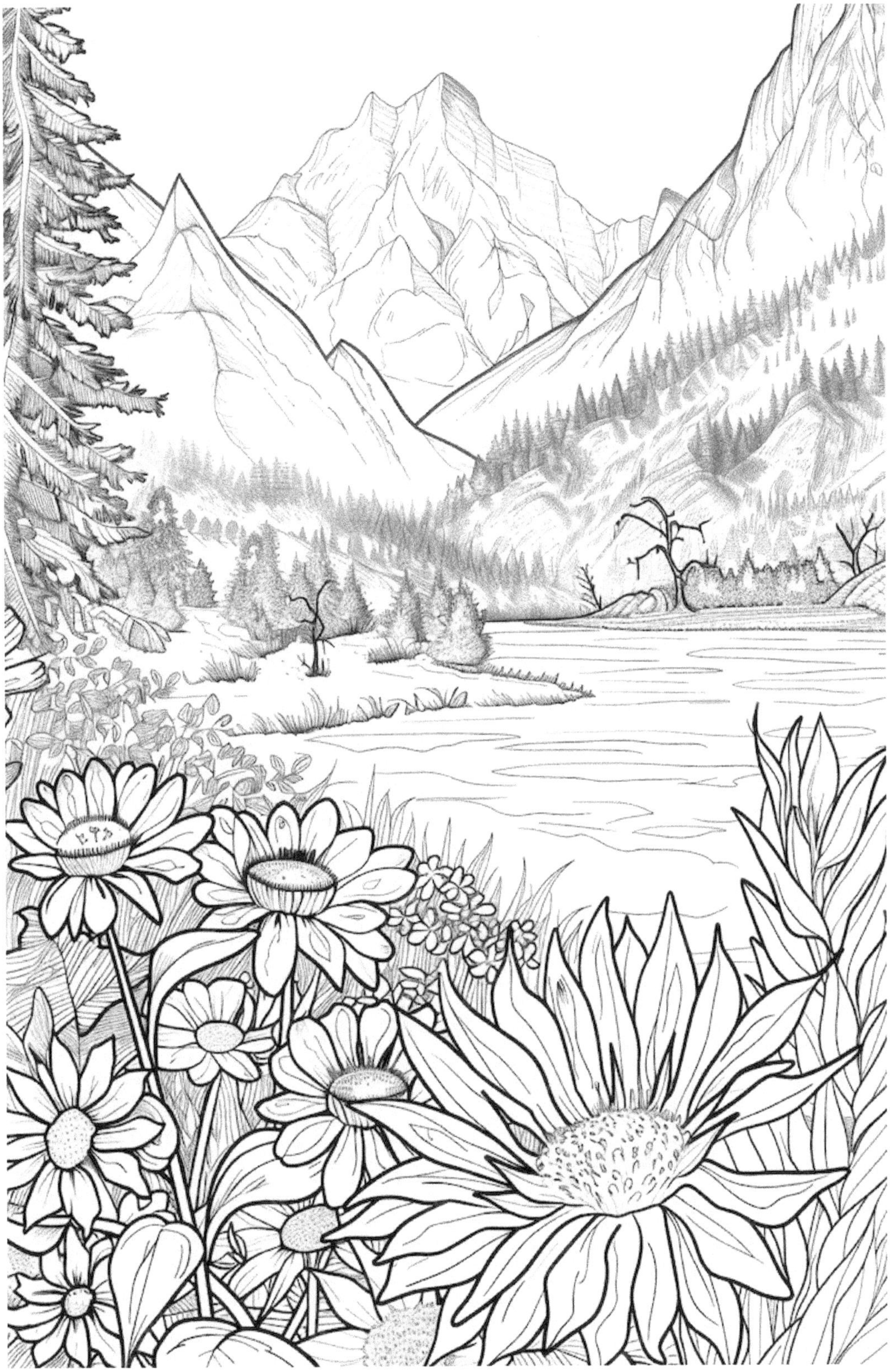

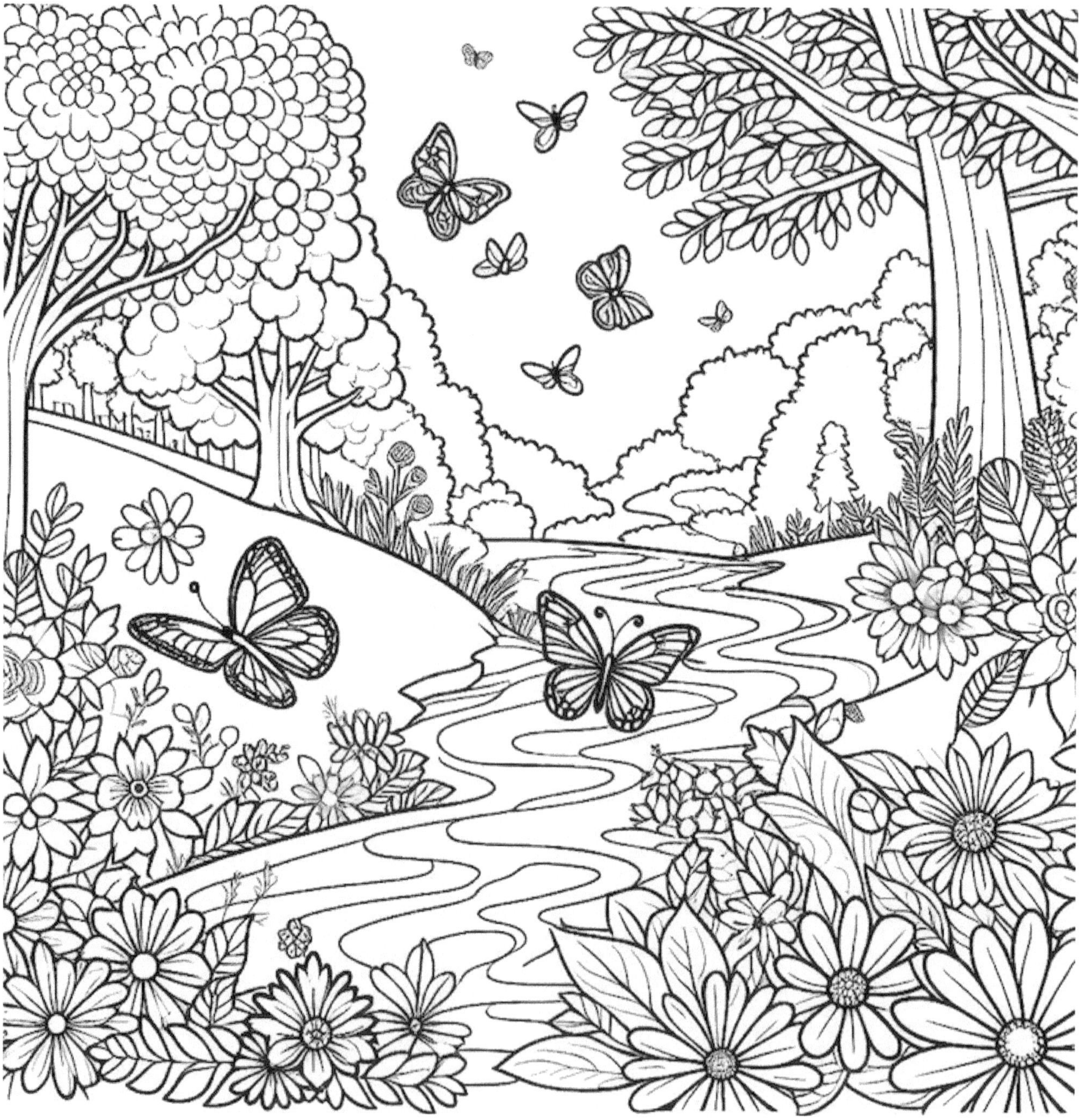

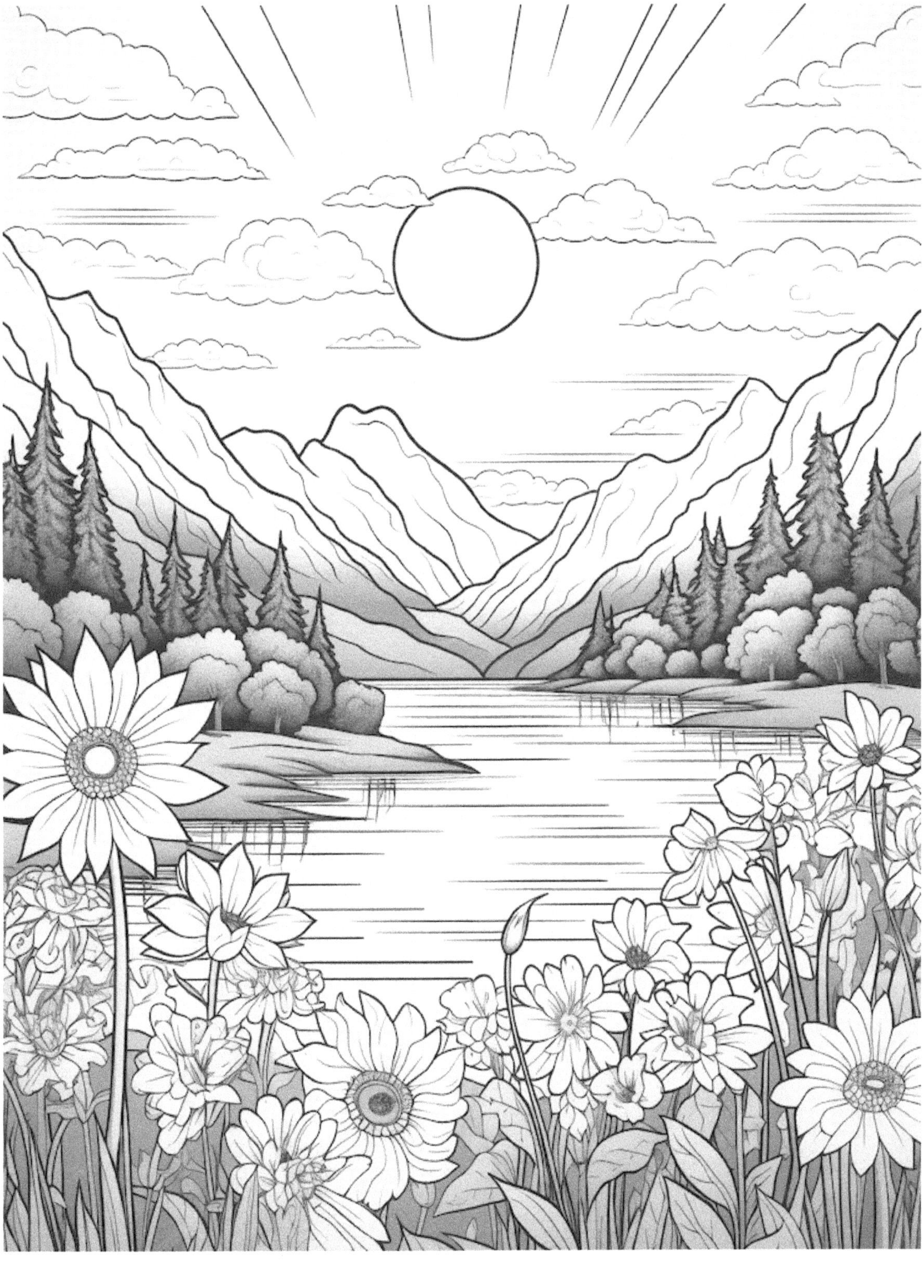

JOURNAL

Capture Feelings, Thoughts, and Dreams through writing

JOURNAL

Capture Feelings, Thoughts, and Dreams through writing

JOURNAL

Capture Feelings, Thoughts, and Dreams through writing

JOURNAL

Capture Feelings, Thoughts, and Dreams through writing

JOURNAL

Capture Feelings, Thoughts, and Dreams through writing

_____

_____

_____

_____

_____

_____

_____

_____

_____

_____

_____

_____

_____

_____

JOURNAL

Capture Feelings, Thoughts, and Dreams through writing

JOURNAL

Capture Feelings, Thoughts, and Dreams through writing

JOURNAL

Capture Feelings, Thoughts, and Dreams through writing

JOURNAL

Capture Feelings, Thoughts, and Dreams through writing

JOURNAL

Capture Feelings, Thoughts, and Dreams through writing

JOURNAL

Capture Feelings, Thoughts, and Dreams through writing

JOURNAL

Capture Feelings, Thoughts, and Dreams through writing

JOURNAL

Capture Feelings, Thoughts, and Dreams through writing

JOURNAL

Capture Feelings, Thoughts, and Dreams through writing

JOURNAL

Capture Feelings, Thoughts, and Dreams through writing

JOURNAL

Capture Feelings, Thoughts, and Dreams through writing

JOURNAL

Capture Feelings, Thoughts, and Dreams through writing

JOURNAL

Capture Feelings, Thoughts, and Dreams through writing

_____

_____

_____

_____

_____

_____

_____

_____

_____

_____

_____

_____

_____

JOURNAL

Capture Feelings, Thoughts, and Dreams through writing

JOURNAL

Capture Feelings, Thoughts, and Dreams through writing

ACTIVITIES

Word Search

```
L S V H I S U R E C O V E R Y
C O G N I T I V E R U F R V S
A L A M I N D F U L N E S S T
T R A U M A N X I E T Y C G R
H G I R E W S U P P O R T B E
P I E V R E S I L I E N C E S
S C H I Z O P H R E N I A C S
Y Y S E V M E D I T A T I O N
C D E P R E S S I O N N T P T
H C O M P A S S I O N W C I H
I D T S S E L F C A R E F N E
A Z K I K B B I P O L A R G R
T C P S Y C H O L O G I S T A
R M G W E L L B E I N G T W P
Y C O U N S E L I N G M A K Y
```

- SCHIZOPHRENIA
- PSYCHOLOGIST
- MINDFULNESS
- DEPRESSION
- RESILIENCE
- COUNSELING
- MEDITATION
- WELLBEING
- COMPASSION
- ANXIETY
- COGNITIVE
- RECOVERY
- SELFCARE
- PSYCHIATRY
- THERAPY
- BIPOLAR
- SUPPORT
- STRESS
- TRAUMA
- COPING

Note: Answer Key located at the end of the book!

Word Search

```
O A X A J M O T Q E F O W U T A G A G S V E F H G D N Q W M
Q Z Z N Z J Z W S M G G G O C H X H W I G K K A M D H D K R
Z U O N G V Z H R B E W V I R Q B E Y O U R S E L F M P J J
C A G I J T P F J O Q S O V S T M B D Y H F H O K E M B L J
C N K B M R B E B D I C Y Y I U H D D X W O U G L P K B W T
L O V E C N G U H Y L Z A U O I U I W G F L A O C R F Y T B
W D D O N Q V D E Q M F Z S J E Y Y N D E M B B S Z J S W A
Y U C E T O C E J B T X L F H K B T P E W Q R X P A C P L E
T K E O S I U C K A Z K W T K F X X H A S G S C T D O F Z D
G B V M T G X G O I A T Z Z R U R H X I U S Q G L I N A P A
E S F M B D J B H M N F Z O W Q K F R V C F U P I X F V F V
B C L J I R K P Y B P D M V X Q O F O K W N N L J O I G K C
O V R X L P A E W W Q A N R O N B S Y F K N F T U G D C Y V
D H Y R G P T C P P O F S E X Z M Z V J O P B X S K E N M K
Y W Z A A U G D E R T U F S S B U A U J C P A M C L N A K M
L G I M K D B E E H R M J Y I S D D K V M D J R J U C B E R
O Q T K D Z I W L Y A Z F T R O B U D I N E S D L W E H N W
V B E T K U U C D R Y F O U U M N Z J R N Q Q X L Y Y Y O J
E Q I A P S O I A Q U N D P X U R O U X C G C H E Z E P U X
D L L C S E F A V L P Y B D M M B L N U L Z P Y V E J P T W
N F V Q C T K T K Y S V P V A T Z V I B A O D E M U A D V B
H N J R Z F B I U B G E O C W Y W E Q F C I S Q A Q I Y F X
Q J S J U R Y L U U T Z L R U B Z R U L F Q O X R C X U Q J
A Z Z N P E V K O D I R A F U Y H S E Y C F M S U Q E H G P
Z M V Q F E W T O R E U B L L J H K L O W R D K N A X X M B
N E I O T D F N V N M A Z R D O S G Y S D D Y L U J K R X I
M X T H E X N G U A J L T D Y Q V K Y S T T D V Q X B P M I
S H M V N B R V M Q N U F S W D T E O L A L N F B K B C D B
G B B E Z Z L H F P B E V A F G W Z U Y E Z P I I N P C I G
X A B H J C T Y J T Q Y U B D T V V A T Y Z V V Z P M Y M M
```

Radical Self-Love	Uniquely You	Making Peace	Love
Compassion	Confidence	Worthiness	
Be Yourself	Kindness	Body Love	
Set Free	Embrace	Enough	
Embody			

Note: Answer Key located at the end of the book!

Word Search

```
A A A K K X M R B W V U T J B J N P D U W A W Y V V Z Y D W
P J L M I H G F Q P H M M Y R R Q R W K Z Q H K J V L Z G S
C X U O Y F A R U X E C Z M E F J A R F E S O E F Q S T Z I
D Y B Y V O O D P S N J S M M Q U T V L F A L S Z D P C H V
C E X Q U I S I T E H Z G R L O A A G D O X E G K T N S D Y
I V B V S V N Q S K F U G V N U P P N L M U H K V D F W H K
I W W S W Q X G Z M O O D N P C V I U Y D X E H T R Y E U T
G I D X T Q O B R W Q A B B L P Q L I M D V A L P Z I E G V
D H M G P F L W O Z D Z B F P N X I V P E G R P Z B H T U K
O J A G U L P E T N Y S L P L X M N G U M F T E V U R N W Z
W I I N O X P O J R J V H G T M Z N X L M H E L H W B E F K
W V S E J W B O P V Z S A W H H W M C O W F D S J E K S R G
F M L A N D J L N P Q W I D M Z R Y F D A N N D Z G J S X D
F Y R L J Z B S T X J H L J S O U I E V A W P N N L I R E V
L E G D V X S W B X U V I B G N A C V H C L A W R X A V M H
W R A N H F B Q B P I X T M M W P E S E Z A J R Y C W S E S
I Y L L F Z Q N J Z U D H S H P M F A A A S V U E W T B R V
Z B X W U O V U T B M N X P R A E O J G C G I F O N J B G S
I K Z R Y S Z W U L U P G P Y O T F A P C R M H O T E W E W
X H Z T O K M K C H E R I S H E D X K U Z J E G A R L S F D
K U P V V T D F B J L Z X V D O U F J F Z K V D A E V T S W
N R I Z J T Y Y C M W D D I A R M M H B C Y C C J A W S J O
K S O U X O X P V A L M S M L B O L J A E R N Q S S Y D F U
P B O D Y P E A C E I Y I U M K V L W Q N L B T A U X O B D
F Z Y Z E J H N D B Q N G Z H V J I M Y B Q I J V R B B A U
U W B Z M G T Z R B N K E C S A Y I V U V D N E Z E J D Q Z
Y Z J R E C L A I M P P V V G H D G Y X J D D M F D Z W L N
P J B R Z T L Y Y U P P N G W G R M B K Z O C Z S T T Q Z P
K P W O A H U N B Z I F M U F E X P A B W W Z J B K Y B B I
Q F T I R R H L X L C W Q X U T C P K T C H C E X U J B G V
```

Wholehearted   Cherished   Treasured
Awareness   Exquisite   Body Peace
Sweetness   Thrive   Belief
Reclaim   Sacred   Loving
Emerge

Note: Answer Key located at the end of the book!

Word Search

```
O J F S O M K G X G X O Q W L E Z Z M C X A N C T B A C P J
Q F C S A N X T L J X B I Q B R X N S B L Y L C Q L B T G Y
Z O N L Z R M Y E N S B Y L Z Q I L V U K M D Q Z R A E L B
P O L Y T Z F R Y S E K M U C J N Z L B P R N M T V D R P E
D W C L L Q G S U E E E F R F U H K N T P P O X B N X V F K
O L J L A G G S S T P N E L I K L W H C M K O W S B U H I J
M D D C A D B Z C P Z G C U N E Y T A T Y D Z R I U K Z I V
Q V M F H I O E U K H H X H K F L J I Q G I V X T F T B G W
E C Q G Z H M R K G D E G O A D M G X V T Z A M S H M T Z U
H P A V Y X X I E G O E G G M N G V G R A W D N Q G M E N O
L Q B R J L T I N W A L Y K I K T O G D S T E G O N Z U L R
W S L H E O H T B G V X T T Y M S I M V E E E K P P W L M B
X F B L R E P D P K S R B F R M Z A N J I O O R A P H S C S
I G E Y B E G A D H J P Y X Q C F M I G M G P I M S Y P V S
O I N Q G V V D S Z P Y A K Q P X O F X R E V C S B L U T I
F B Z Q J Q T E G S O V K C K M D X R J B Q Q S F Z P S Z I
W S A X I T B B R N I Q A N E V T R P Y W H E G R O X Y G D
N N N O U R I S H E K O L M S C P G G U V P G S V X G D N G
F N P U W D Z L J H N A N Y B G S A F S C J L F M S K E F A
Q G U J L T B W R J P C H J Z I C X O G O Z U Z O H P C B M
B F V R S W O S W Z F O E G B G W J V H I S N W D C Q R U I
K A G H T D W O G B M P V X F W U Y T C A U J D X R Y A I O
Y W L Q C U W H Q D S N U L U J V W A O Q Y B S F V K G V T
R E L G K F R H W E K M C Z H G U K D V G L T N R F F N W N
E R J L W F P E Z V G U K Y L A M P A Y E C N F R J I E W H
P L R Y P H O Q X O W B F J F S K I B R Y A K Q K B Z E I U
R A D I A N C E E T S E L F A C C E P T A N C E U V N O T S
C C R S H I N E C E Q N T T M L G T P Z A K L C W X T Y D I
F B G C R Q V C W D K F J M P H A H E V G T H J V F H C E O
A C P B C K D A R P G H J R P J W M V J V B C V G W R S Q P
```

Self-Acceptance	Claiming Space	Enchanting	Care
Cultivate	Reverence	Radiance	
Passion	Devoted	Nourish	
Support	Shine	Nurture	
Adore			

Note: Answer Key located at the end of the book!

SUNDAY:

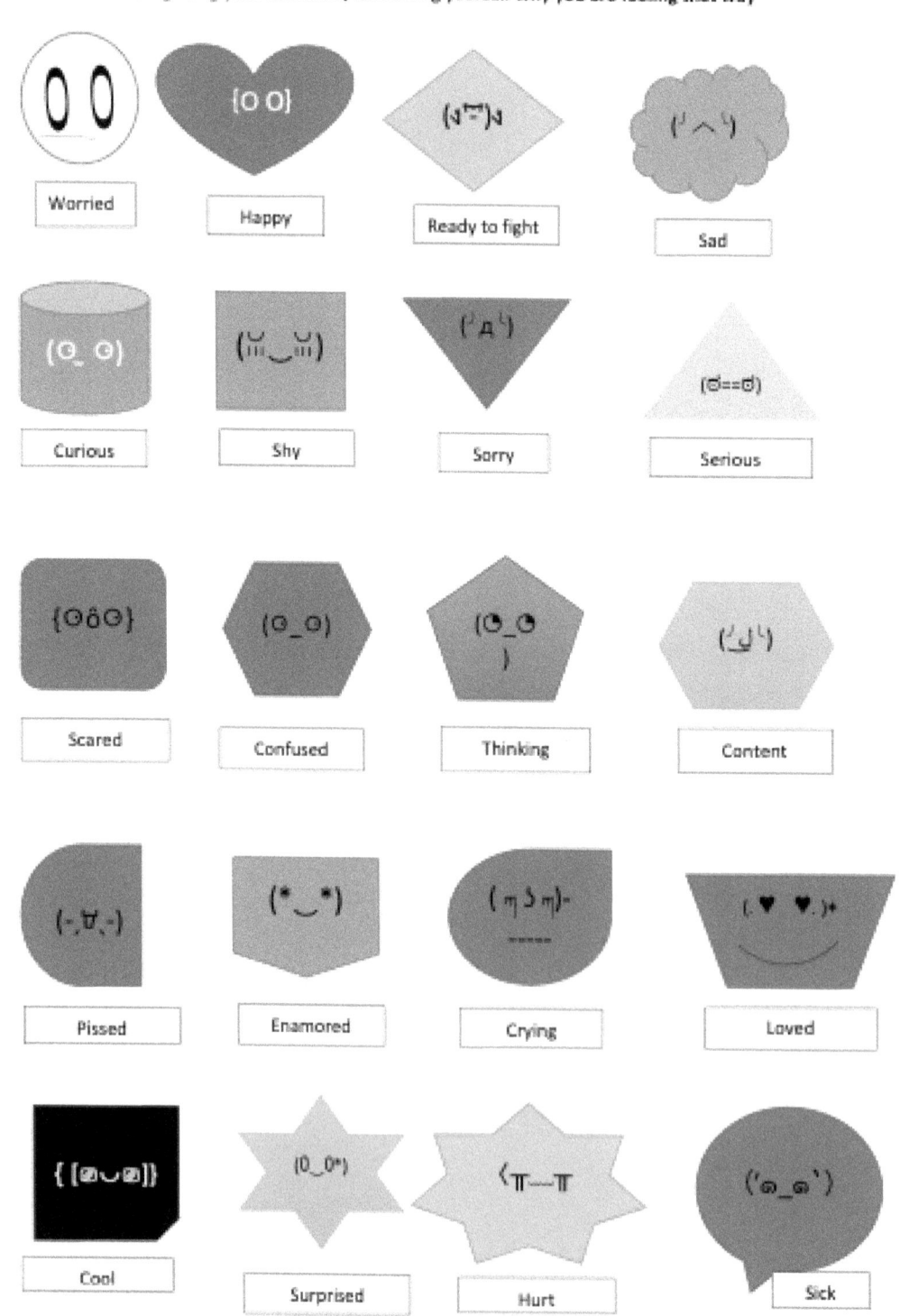

Recognizing your emotions, and asking yourself why you are feeling that way

{O O}	Worried
{O O}	Happy
(৶ ̄ˇ ̄)৶	Ready to fight
(´︵`)	Sad
(O_O)	Curious
(ⅲ‿ⅲ)	Shy
(´д`)	Sorry
(๏==๏)	Serious
{OôO}	Scared
(O_O)	Confused
(◔_◔)	Thinking
(´⌣`)	Content
(-.ѱ.-)	Pissed
(*‿*)	Enamored
(ηЗη)-	Crying
(.♥ ♥.)+	Loved
{[๏‿๏]}	Cool
(0_0*)	Surprised
⟨π—π	Hurt
('๏_๏')	Sick

106

MONDAY:

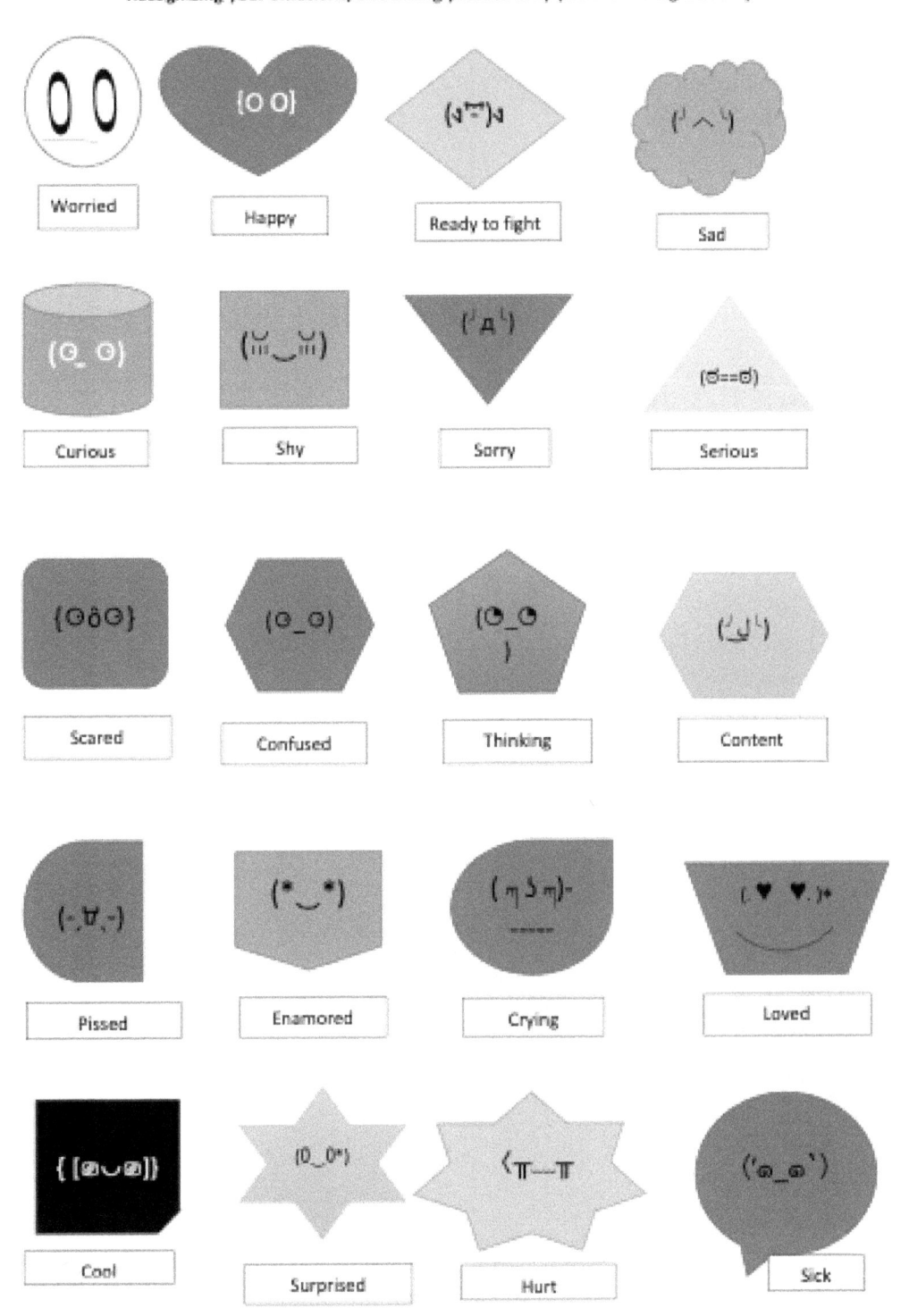

Recognizing your emotions, and asking yourself why you are feeling that way

Worried	Happy	Ready to fight	Sad
Curious	Shy	Sorry	Serious
Scared	Confused	Thinking	Content
Pissed	Enamored	Crying	Loved
Cool	Surprised	Hurt	Sick

TUESDAY:

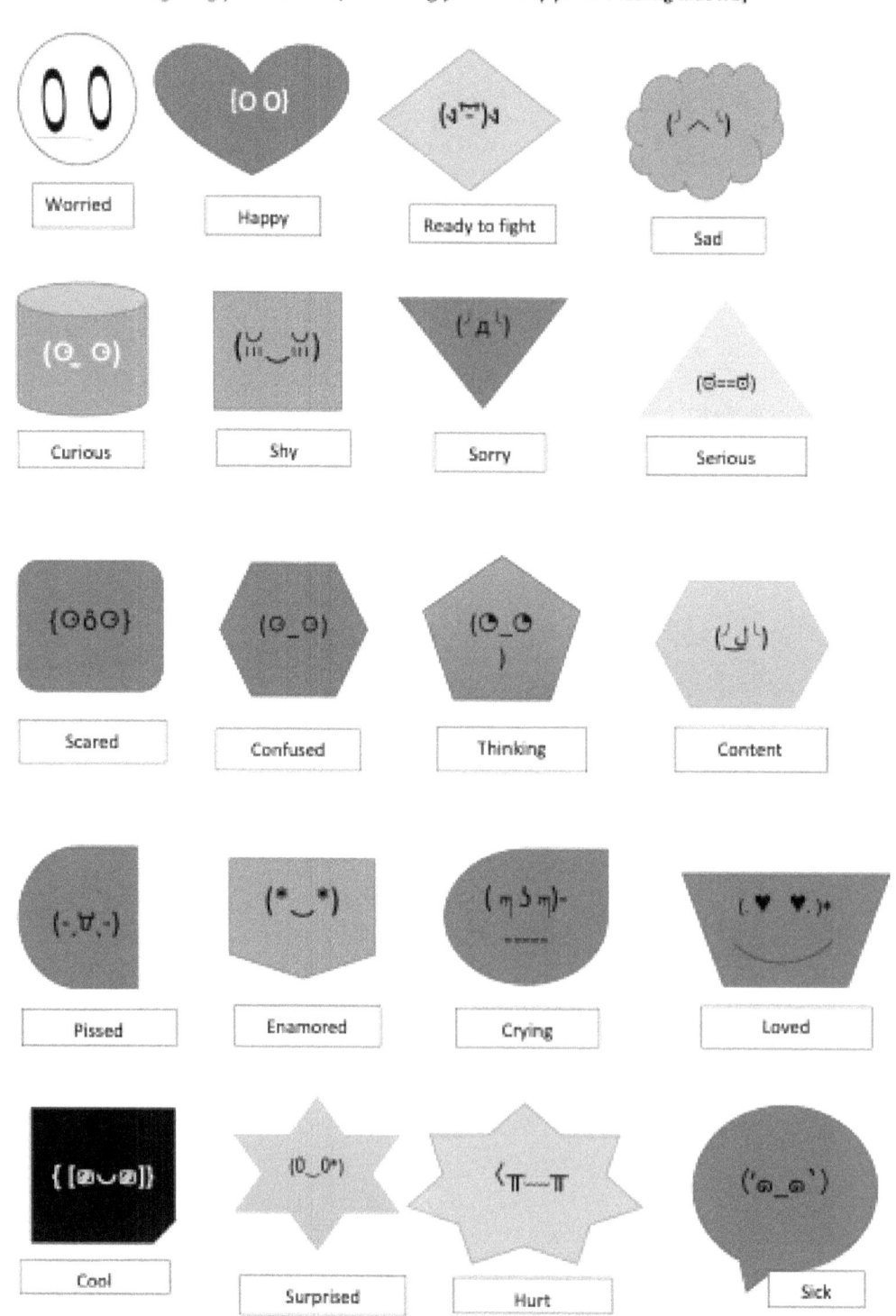

Recognizing your emotions, and asking yourself why you are feeling that way

Worried	Happy	Ready to fight	Sad
Curious	Shy	Sorry	Serious
Scared	Confused	Thinking	Content
Pissed	Enamored	Crying	Loved
Cool	Surprised	Hurt	Sick

108

WEDNESDAY:

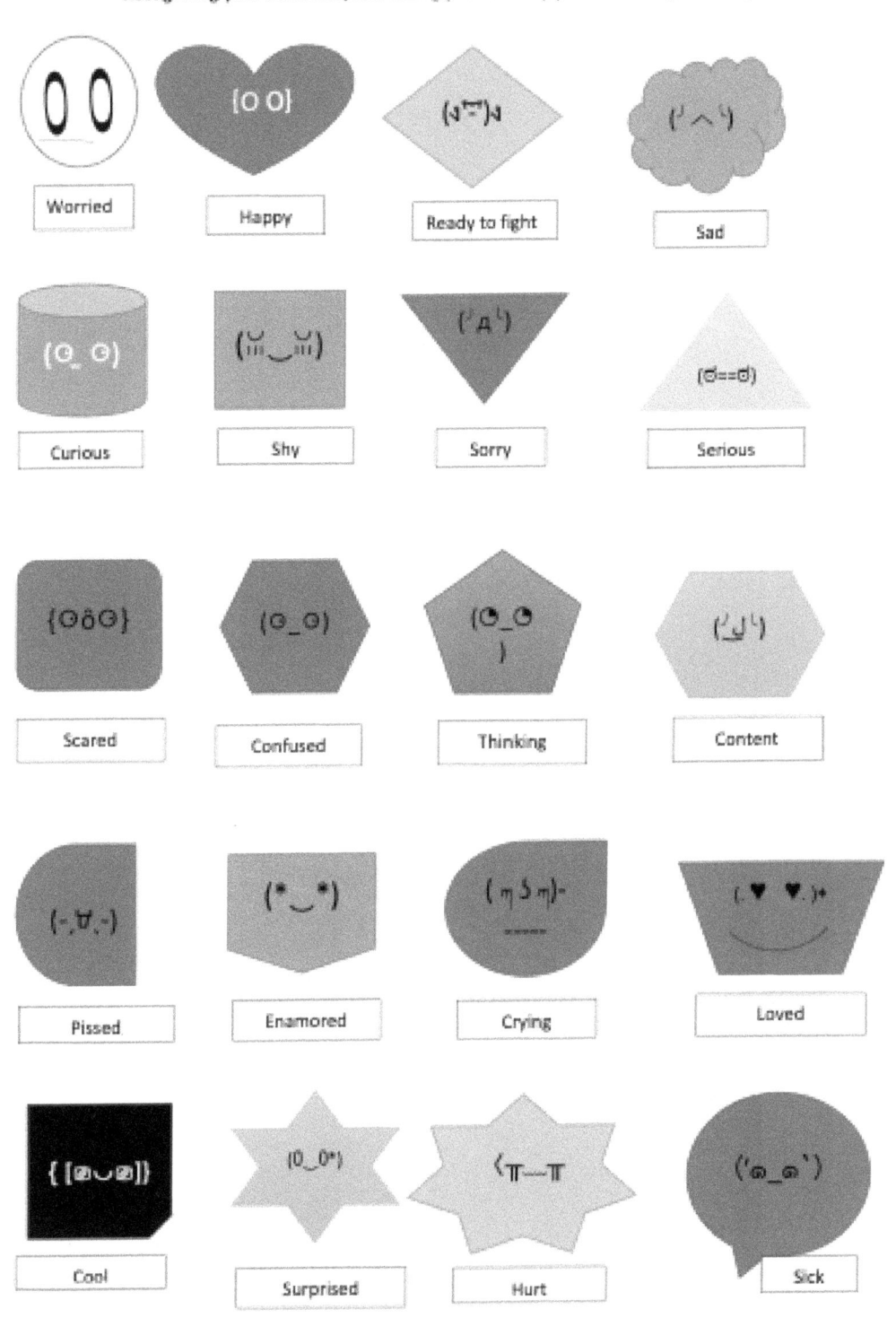

Recognizing your emotions, and asking yourself why you are feeling that way

Worried	Happy	Ready to fight	Sad
Curious	Shy	Sorry	Serious
Scared	Confused	Thinking	Content
Pissed	Enamored	Crying	Loved
Cool	Surprised	Hurt	Sick

THURSDAY:

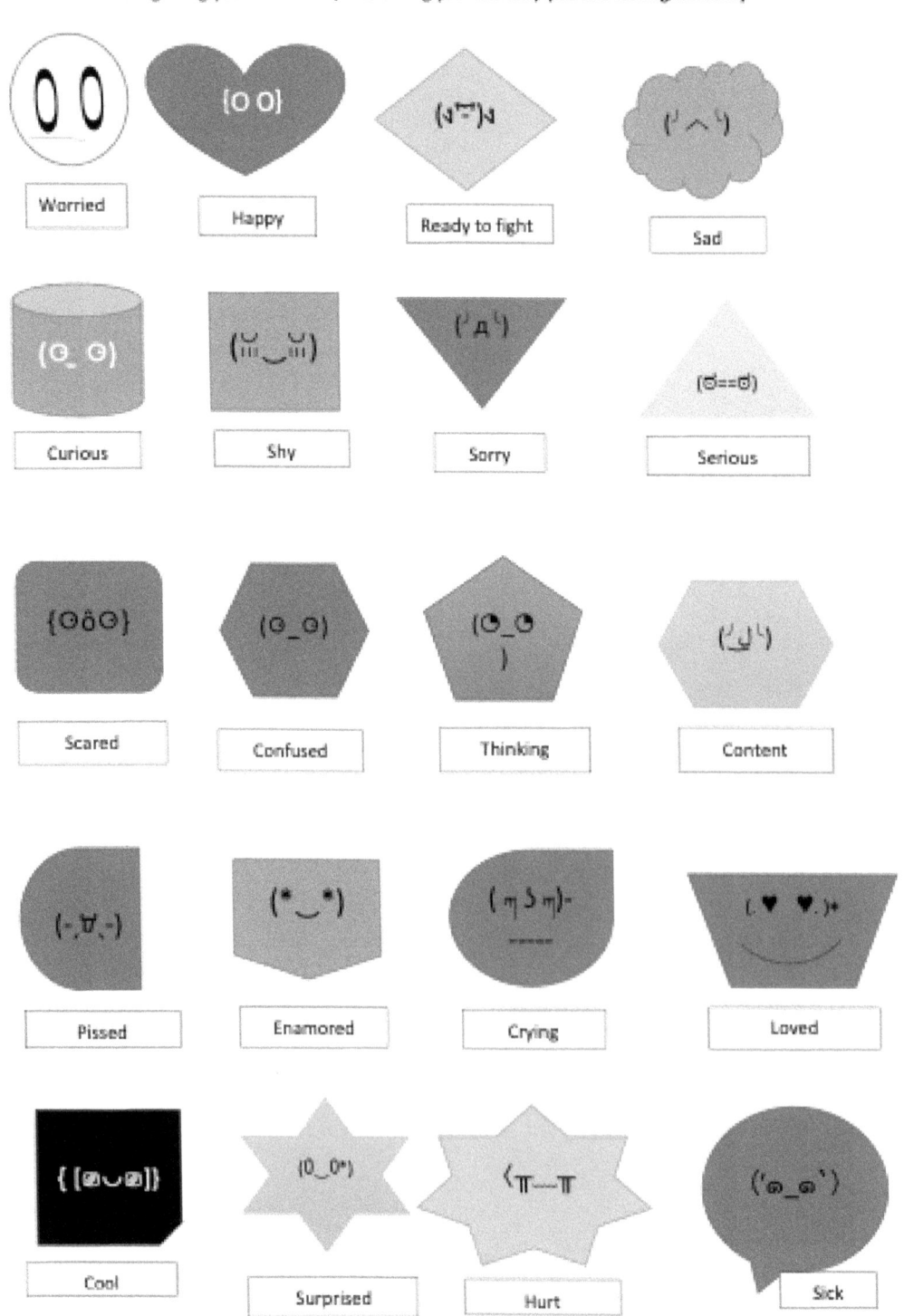

Recognizing your emotions, and asking yourself why you are feeling that way

(O O)	Worried
{O O}	Happy
(ง ͠° ͟ʖ ͡°)ง	Ready to fight
(╯︵╰)	Sad
(☉_☉)	Curious
(⊌‿⊌)	Shy
(╥﹏╥)	Sorry
(⌐■==■)	Serious
{⊙ȯ⊙}	Scared
(⊙_⊙)	Confused
(◔_◔)	Thinking
(´ᴗ`)	Content
(-.¤.-)	Pissed
(*‿*)	Enamored
(η ⊃ η)-	Crying
(.♥ ♥.)+	Loved
{[⊘‿⊘]}	Cool
(0_0*)	Surprised
‹π—π	Hurt
('๏_๏')	Sick

FRIDAY:

Recognizing your emotions, and asking yourself why you are feeling that way

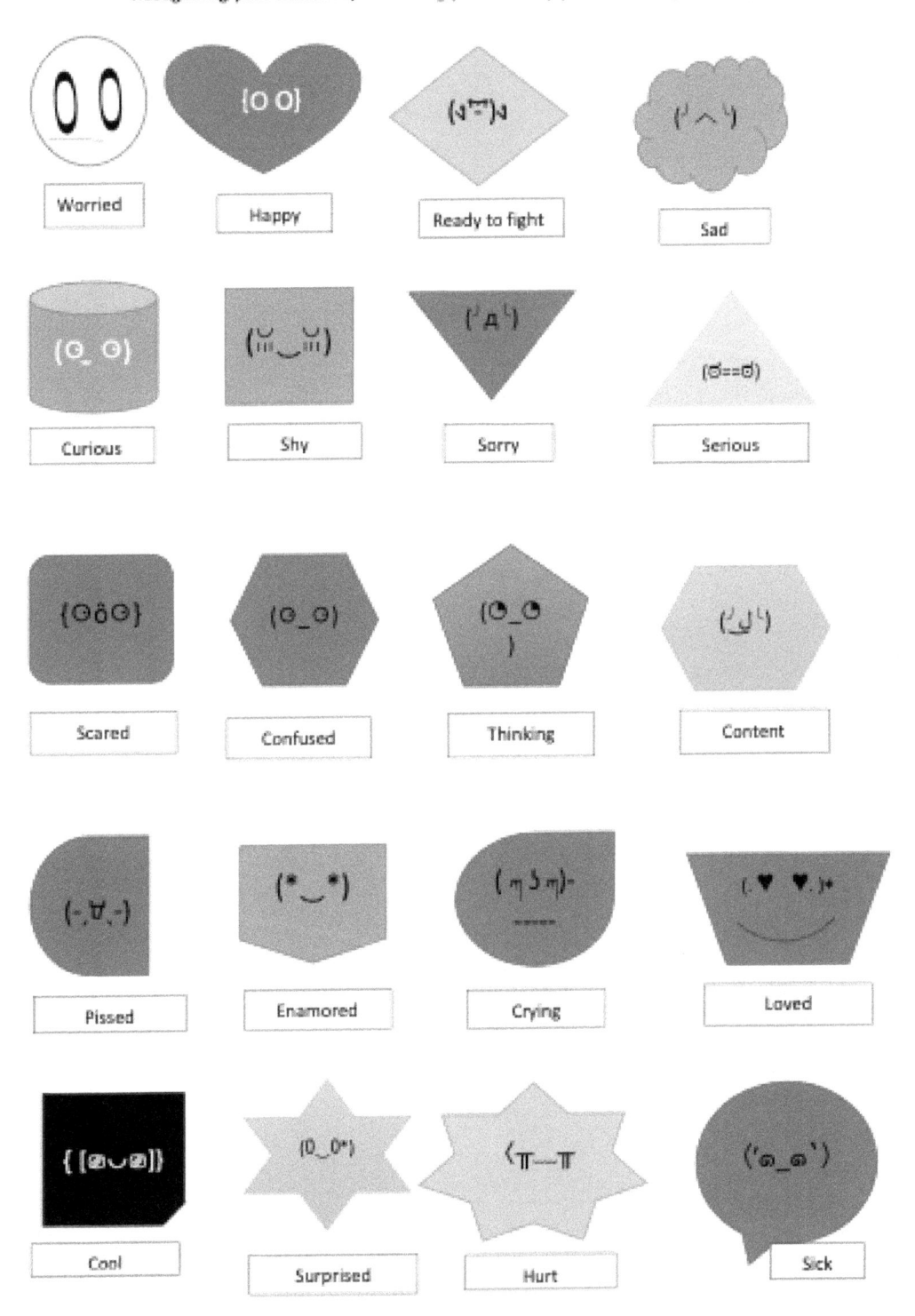

Worried	Happy	Ready to fight	Sad
Curious	Shy	Sorry	Serious
Scared	Confused	Thinking	Content
Pissed	Enamored	Crying	Loved
Cool	Surprised	Hurt	Sick

SATURDAY:

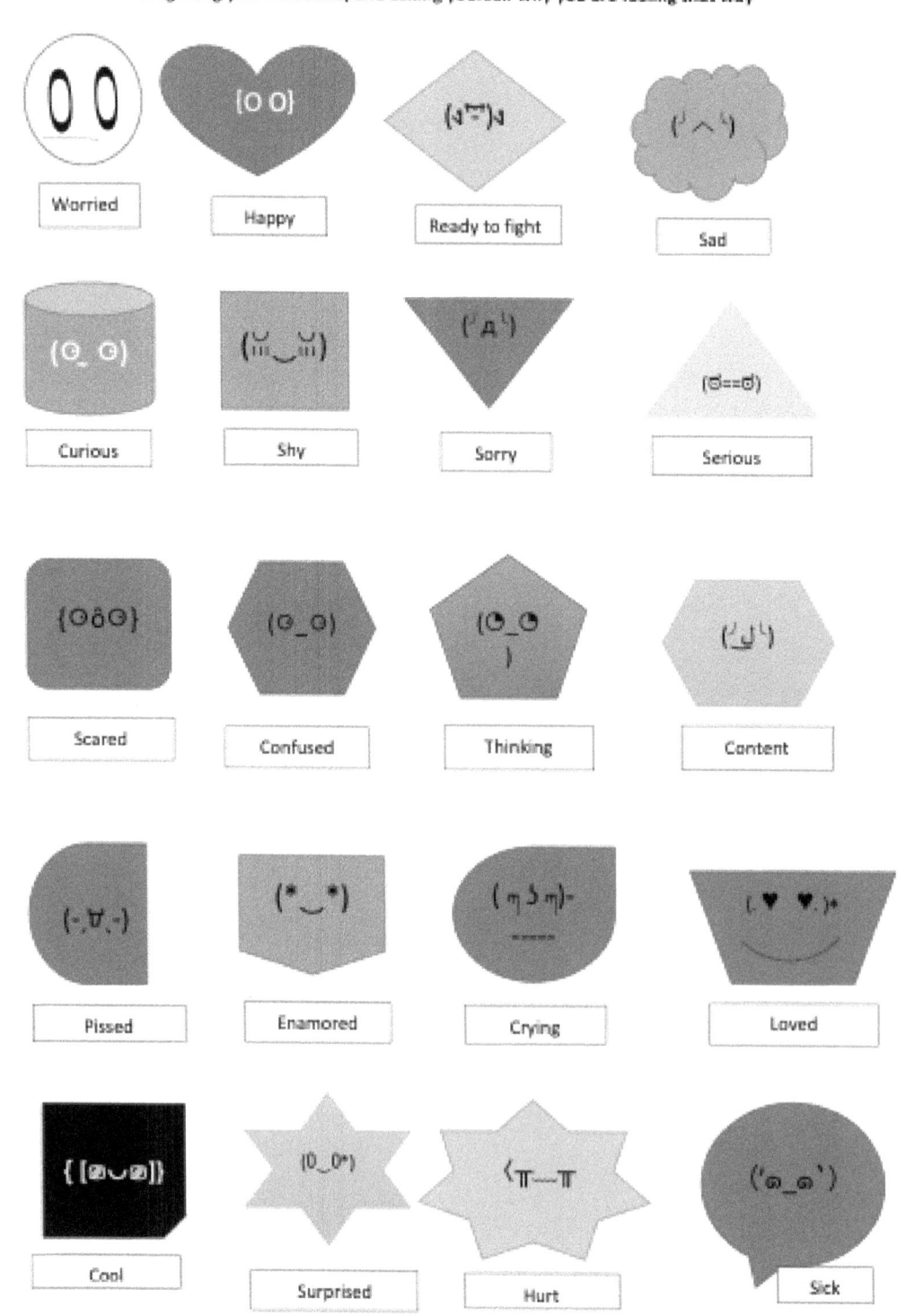

Recognizing your emotions, and asking yourself why you are feeling that way

Worried	Happy	Ready to fight	Sad
Curious	Shy	Sorry	Serious
Scared	Confused	Thinking	Content
Pissed	Enamored	Crying	Loved
Cool	Surprised	Hurt	Sick

LAUGHTER IS GOOD FOR THE HEART

1. A man walks into a library and asks the librarian for books about paranoia. She whispers, "They're right behind you!"

2. Want to hear a roof joke? The first one's on the house.

3. What should you do if you're attacked by a group of clowns? Go straight for the juggler.

4. I saw a movie about how ships are put together. It was riveting.

5. Why did the taxi driver get fired? Passengers didn't like it when she went the extra mile.

6. How do you look for Will Smith in the snow? Just follow the fresh prints.

7. I couldn't believe that the highway department called my dad a thief. But when I got home, all the signs were there.

8. I submitted 10 puns to a joke-writing competition to see if any of them made the finals. Sadly, no pun in 10 did.

9. Which rock group has four guys who can't sing or play instruments? Mount Rushmore.

10. Why does Humpty Dumpty love autumn? Because he always has a great fall.

11. It's always windy in a sports arena. All those fans.

12. Why should you never trust stairs? They're always up to something.

13. How do mountains stay warm in the winter? Snowcaps.

14. Is this pool safe for diving? It deep ends.

15. I tried to catch fog yesterday. I mist.

16. What do you call a religious person who sleepwalks? A roamin' Catholic.

17. Two windmills are standing on a wind farm. One asks, "What's your favorite kind of music?" The other replies, "I'm a big metal fan."

18. What kind of shorts do clouds wear? Thunder pants.

19. Can February March? No, but April May.

20. What is red and smells like blue paint? Red paint.

21. What do dentists call their x-rays? Tooth pics.

22. What's the difference between a poorly dressed man on a unicycle and a well-dressed man on a bicycle? Attire.

23. What is the best day to go to the beach? Sunday, of course.

24. What bow can't be tied? A rainbow.

25. People think "icy" is the easiest word to spell. Come to think of it, I see why.

26. My teachers told me I'd never amount to much because I procrastinate so much. I told them, "Just you wait!"

27. What's a foot long and slippery? A slipper.

28. What do we want? Low-flying airplane noises! When do we want them? NEEEEYYYOOOOOOOOWWWW!

29. What building in New York has the most stories? The public library.

30. Comic Sans walks into a bar. The bartender says, "We don't serve your type here."

31. What's the easiest way to get straight As? Use a ruler.

32. What's a balloon's least favorite type of music? Pop.

33. Did you hear about the painter who was hospitalized? The doctors say it was due to too many strokes.

34. What washes up on very small beaches? Micro-waves.

35. How does a farmer mend his overalls? With cabbage patches.

36. I got my husband a fridge for his birthday. His face lit up when he opened it.

37. Why were they called the Dark Ages? Because there were lots of knights.

38. How does NASA organize a party? They planet.

39. What did the big flower say to the little flower? "Hi bud!"

40. How did the hipster burn his mouth? He ate his pizza before it was cool.

41. Why is no one friends with Dracula? Because he's a pain in the neck.

42. Wanna hear two short jokes and a long joke? Joke, joke, jooooooooooooke.

43. What do Alexander the Great and Winnie the Pooh have in common? The same middle name.

44. I bought the world's worst thesaurus yesterday. Not only is it terrible, it's terrible.

45. A man walks into a library and orders a hamburger. The librarian says, "This is a library." The man apologizes and whispers, "I'd like a hamburger, please."

46. Where do hamburgers take their sweethearts on Valentine's Day to dance? The Meat Ball.

47. Some people eat snails. They must not like fast food.

48. Have you heard about Murphy's Law? Yes. Anything that can go wrong will go wrong. How about Cole's Law? No. It's julienned cabbage in a creamy dressing.

49. What did the green grape say to the purple grape? "Breathe, man! Breathe!"

50. What do you call a fake noodle? An impasta.

51. Did you hear about the cheese factory that exploded in France? There was nothing left but de-Brie.

52. What is the resemblance between a green apple and a red apple? They're both red except for the green one.

53. Did you hear about the first restaurant to open on the moon? It had great food, but no atmosphere.

54. Why did the tomato blush? Because it saw the salad dressing.

55. What did the Buddhist say to the hot dog vendor? "Make me one with everything."

56. What do you get when you pour root beer into a square cup? Beer.

https://bestlifeonline.com/funny-clean-jokes/ Sarah Crow is a senior editor at Eat This, Not That! where she focuses on celebrity news and health coverage.

WORD SEARCH ANSWER KEYS

Word Search

```
L S V H I S U R E C O V E R Y
C O G N I T I V E R U F R V S
A L A M I N D F U L N E S S T
T R A U M A N X I E T Y C G R
H G I R E W S U P P O R T B E
P I E V R E S I L I E N C E S
S C H I Z O P H R E N I A C S
Y Y S E V M E D I T A T I O N
C D E P R E S S I O N N T P T
H C O M P A S S I O N W C I H
I D T S S E L F C A R E F N E
A Z K I K B B I P O L A R G R
T C P S Y C H O L O G I S T A
R M G W E L L B E I N G T W P
Y C O U N S E L I N G M A K Y
```

- SCHIZOPHRENIA
- DEPRESSION
- MEDITATION
- ANXIETY
- SELFCARE
- BIPOLAR
- TRAUMA
- PSYCHOLOGIST
- RESILIENCE
- WELLBEING
- COGNITIVE
- PSYCHIATRY
- SUPPORT
- COPING
- MINDFULNESS
- COUNSELING
- COMPASSION
- RECOVERY
- THERAPY
- STRESS

Word Search

```
O A X A J M O T Q E F O W U T A G A G S V E F H G D N Q W M
Q Z Z N Z J Z W S M G G O C H X H W I G K K A M D H D K R
Z U O N G V Z H R B E W V I R O B E Y O U R S E L F M P J J
C A G I J T P F J O Q S O V S T M B D Y H F H O K E M B L J
C N K B M R B E B D I C Y Y I U H D D X W O U G L P K B W T
L O V E C N G U H Y L Z A U O I U I W G F L A O C R F Y T B
W D D O N O V D E Q M F Z S J E Y Y N D E M B B S Z J S W A
Y U C E T O C E J B T X L F H K B T P E W Q R X P A C P L E
T K E O S I U C K A Z K W T K F X X H A S G S C T D O F Z D
G B V M T G X G O I A T Z Z R U R H X I U S Q G L I N A P A
E S F M B D J B H M N F Z O W Q K F R V C F U P I X F V F V
B C L J I R K P Y B P D M V X Q O F O K W N N L J O I G K C
O V R X L P A E W W Q A W R O N B S Y F K N F T U G D C V X
D H Y R G P T C P P O F S E X Z M Z V J O P B X S K E N M K
Y W Z A A U G E R T U F S S B U A U J C P A M C L N A K M
L G I M K D B E E H R M J Y S D D K V M D J R J U C B E R
O Q T K D Z I W L Y A Z F T R O B U D I N E S D L W E H N W
V B E T K U U C D R Y F O U U M N Z J R N Q Q X L Y Y O J
E Q I A P S O I A Q U N D P X U R O U X C G C H E Z E P U X
D L L C S E F A V L P Y B D M M B L N U L Z P Y V E J P T W
N F V Q C T K T K Y S V P V A T Z V I B A O D E M U A D V B
H N J R Z F B I U B G E Q C W Y W E Q F C I S Q A Q I Y F X
Q J S J U R Y L U U T Z L R U B Z R U L F Q O X R C X U Q J
A Z Z N P E V K O D I R A F U Y H S E Y C F M S U Q D H G P
Z M V Q F E W T O R E U B L L H K L O W R D K N A X X M B
N E I O T D F N V N M A Z R D O S G Y S D D Y L U J K R X I
M X T H E X N G U A J L T D Y Q V K Y S T T D V Q X B P M I
S H M V N B R V M Q N U F S W D T E O L A L N F B K B C D B
G B B E Z Z L H F P B E V A F G W Z U Y E Z P I I N P C I G
X A B H J C T Y J T Q Y U B D T V V A T Y Z V V Z P M Y M M
```

Radical Self-Love   Uniquely You   Making Peace   Love

Compassion   Confidence   Worthiness

Be Yourself   Kindness   Body Love

Set Free   Embrace   Enough

Embody

Word Search

```
A A A K K X M R B W V U T J B J N P D U W A W Y V V Z Y D W
P J L M I H G F Q P H M M Y R R Q R W K Z Q H K J V L Z G S
C X U O Y F A R U X E Z F J A R F E S O E F Q S T Z I
D Y B Y W O O D P S N J S M M Q U T V L F A L S Z D P C H V
C E X Q U I S I T E H Z G R L O A A G D O X E G K T N S D Y
I V B V S V N Q S K F U G V N U P H N L M U H K V D F W H K
I W W S W Q X G Z M O O D N P C V I U Y D X E H T R Y E U T
G I D X T Q O B R W Q A B B L P Q L I M D V A L P Z I E G V
D H M G P F L W O Z D B F P N X I V P E G R P Z B H T U K
O J A G U L P E T N Y S L P L X M N G U M F T E V U R N W Z
W I I N O X P O J R J V H G T M Z N X L M H E L H W B E F K
W V S E J W B O P V Z S A W H H W M C O W F D S J E K S R G
F M L A N D J L N P Q W I D M Z R Y F D A N N D Z G J S X D
F Y R L J Z B S T X J H L J S O U E V A W P N N L I R E V
L E G D V X S W B X U V I B G N A C V H C L A W R X A V M H
W R A N H F B Q B P I X T M M W P E S E Z A J R Y C W S E S
I Y L L F Z Q N J Z U D H S H P M F A A S V U E W T B R V
Z B X W U O V U T B M N X P R A E O J G C G I F O N I B G S
I K Z R Y S Z W U L U P G P Y O T F A P C R M H O T E W E W
X H Z T O K M K C H E R I S H E D X K U Z J E G A R L S F D
K U P V V T D F B J L Z K V D O U F J F Z K V D A E V T S W
N R I Z J T Y Y C M W D D I A R M M H B C Y C C J A W S J O
K S O U X O X P V A L M S M L B O L J A E R N Q S S Y D F U
P B O D Y P E A C E I Y I U M K V L W Q N L B T A U X O B D
F Z Y Z E J H N D B Q N G Z H V J I M Y B O J V R B B A U
U W B Z M G T Z R B N K E C S A Y I V U V D N E Z J D Q Z
Y Z J R E C L A I M P P V V G H D Q G Y X J D D M F D Z W L N
P J B R Z T L Y Y U P P N G W G R M B K Z O C Z S T T Q Z P
K P W O A H U N B Z I F M U F E X P A B W W Z J B K Y B B I
Q F T I R R H L X L C W Q X U T C P K T C H C E X U J B G V
```

Wholehearted   Cherished   Treasured
Awareness   Exquisite   Body Peace
Sweetness   Thrive   Belief
Reclaim   Sacred   Loving
Emerge

Word Search

```
O J F S O M K G X O Q W L E Z Z M C X A N C T B A C P J
Q F C S A N X T L J X B I Q B R X N S B L Y L C Q L B T G Y
Z O N L Z R M Y E N S B Y L Z Q I L V U K M D Q Z R A E L B
P O L Y T Z F R Y S E K M U C J N Z L B P R N M T V D R P E
D W C L L Q G S U E E F R F U H K N T P O X B N X V F K
O L J L A G G S S T P N E L L W H C M K O W S B U H I J
M D D C A D B Z C P Z G C U N E Y T A T Y D Z R J U K Z I V
Q V M F H N O E U K H H X H K F L J I Q G I V X T F T B G W
E C O G Z H M R K G D E G O A D M G X V T Z A M S H M T Z U
H P A V Y X X I E G O E G G M N G V G R A W D N Q G M E N O
L Q B R J L T I N W A L Y K I K T O G D S T E G O N Z U L R
W S L H E O H T B G V X T T Y M S I M V E E D K P P W L M B
X F B L R E D P K S R B F R M Z A N J O O R A P H S C S
I G E Y B E G A D H J P Y X Q C F M I G M G P I M S Y P V S
O I N Q G V D S Z P Y A K Q P X O F X R E V C S B L U T I
F B Z Q J Q T E G S O V K C K M D X R J B Q Q S F Z P S Z I
W S A X I T B B R N I O A N E V T R P Y W H E G R O X Y G D
N N N O U R I S H E K O L M S C P G G U V P G S V X G D N G
F N P U W D Z L J H N A N Y B G S A F S C J L F M S K E F A
Q G U L T B W R J P C H J Z I C X O G O Z U Z O H P C B M
B F V R S W O S W Z F O E G B G W J V H I S N W D C Q R U I
K A G H T D W O G B M P V X F W U Y T C A U J D X R Y A I O
Y W L Q C W H Q D S N U L U J V W A O Q Y B S F V K G V T
R E L G K R H W E K M C Z H G U K D V G L T N R F F N W N
E R J L W F P E Z V G U K Y L A M P A Y E C N F R J I E W H
P L R Y P H O Q X O W B F J F S K I B R Y A K Q K B Z E I U
R A D I A N C E E T S E L F A C C E P T A N C E U V N O T S
C C R S H I N E C E Q N T T M L G T P Z A K L C W X T Y D I
F B G C R Q V C W D K F J M P H A H E V G T H J V F H C E O
A C P B C K D A R P G H J R P J W M V J V B C V G W R S Q P
```

Self-Acceptance	Claiming Space	Enchanting	Care
Cultivate	Reverence	Radiance	
Passion	Devoted	Nourish	
Support	Shine	Nurture	
Adore